Commission of the European

science and technology policy

Organization, people and technology in European manufacturing

P. Kidd

**Cheshire Henbury
Research & Consultancy**
Tamworth House
PO Box 103
Macclesfield, Cheshire SK11 8UW
United Kingdom

Contract No MOFA-0004-D (MB)

Final report

Directorate-General
Science, Research and Development

1992

EUR 13967 EN

Published by the
COMMISSION OF THE EUROPEAN COMMUNITIES
Directorate-General
Telecommunications, Information Industries and Innovation
L-2920 Luxembourg

LEGAL NOTICE

Neither the Commission of the European Communities nor any person acting on behalf of the Commission is responsible for the use which might be made of the following information

Cataloguing data can be found at the end of this publication

Luxembourg: Office for Official Publications of the European Communities, 1992

ISBN 92-826-3819-7

© ECSC-EEC-EAEC, Brussels • Luxembourg, 1992

Printed in France

PREFACE

Since the mid 1970's industry in Europe has performed less well in comparison with the USA and especially compared to Japan. Europe has also lost ground in basic research where its spending on R & D (as a percentage of GDP) is below both the USA and Japan. However, the completion of the single market by the end of 1992 and the future prospect of an enlarged Community of EC16, or 18+ by the 21st century offers the potential for a resurgence in European manufacturing. Collectively, the papers in this series demonstrate how anthropocentric production systems can fulfill this potential. Based upon extensive research on the various sectors and regions of European manufacturing, the different reports converge towards a common conclusion: that reliance upon technology alone is an inadequate response to the challanges of world markets in the future; that successful modernisation of European industry depends upon its most valuable resource - human skills and creativity.

This report is part of a publication series presenting the results of FAST research on the "prospects and conditions for anthropocentric production systems in Europe by the 21st Century". The research was sponsored by the European Commission MONITOR - FAST Programme, 1989-1992 and generously co-funded by the government of Nordrhein Westfalen in the Federal Republic of Germany. Research teams from all countries of the European Community participated in the project, as well as researchers from the USA, Japan and Australia. More than twenty reports are available or in the process of publication providing a comprehensive and comparative assessment of the human aspects of advanced manufacturing in Europe.

All of the studies in the series address the general issue of defining anthropocentric production systems: national research traditions and manufacturing experience in the various member states have produced different interpretations of anthropocentric production systems; this is regarded as a strength not a weakness of European manufacturing in the sense that European diversity suggests a number of possible trajectories of change in manufacturing in response to world competition in the 1990's rather than a unilinear path of development, or an assumption that there is "one best way" of managing technological change. A central feature of the research was close collaboration between the research teams and workshop discussions: this helped to identify a common minimal definition of anthropocentric production systems and a common analytical framework for country comparisons without the straitjacket of a predetermined research schema which would have lacked sensitivity to cultural differences in Europe.

APS can be defined as advanced manufacturing based on the optimal utilisation of skilled human resources, collaborative industrial organisation and adapted technologies. All the reports in the series explore the concept of APS in some detail, especially the general reports by Werner Wobbe - series no. 1, Paul Kidd - series no. 3 and Franz Lehner - series no. 4.

The reports comprise the research results of four networks:

The first - country studies co-ordinated by the Institut Arbeit Technik, Gelsenkirchen. It included social scientists from the member states who are to investigate the socioeconomic factors which affect the prospects and conditions for APS by the early 21st Century. This included, in addition, a synthesis report, comparing the research results from the various member states (Franz Lehner, Report no. 4) and special consideration of the less industrialized member states (coordinated by Sean O'Siochru, NEXUS, Ireland: Report no. 6).

Secondly, a Technical Recommendations Network, coordinated by P. Kidd (Cheshire - Henbury), comprising technical experts, who addressed the interface between the technical features of advanced manufacturing and human resources in order to identify future research priorities for the European Commission (Report no.3).

A third network, coordinated by D. Brandt (HDZ, Aachen), undertook a survey of case studies of the application of APS in the member states (Report no. 2).

Fourthly, the CAPIRN Network (Culture and Production International Research Network) coordinated by Felix Rauner (Bremen) and Richard Gordon (Santa Cruz), reports on the results of an international project on production cultures, comparing Europe with Japan, USA, and Australia and situating its analysis in the context of Anthropocentric Production Systems.

The series also includes a number of related studies of specific issues concerning the implications of APS for technology design.

KEY ISSUES

1. Dynamic markets, increased product variety and changed cost structures require new approaches and new ideas in manufacturing.

2. In the past manufacturing has been cost driven and technology has provided an important means of reducing costs.

3. Manufacturing now needs a more balanced approach based on organisation, people and technology because cost reduction is not the sole criteria for competitive manufacturing.

4. European Commission funded research in the area of advanced manufacturing needs to be more broadly based.

5. There are many research areas in manufacturing which need an interdisciplinary approach.

6. Organisation and people issues in manufacturing are not just about man-machine interfaces, or smoothing the way for more technology, or the quality of working life, or health and safety, or job satisfaction.

7. Technology is not the only or prime source of increased competitiveness. The skills, judgement and experience of highly motivated people can also contribute to improving competitiveness.

8. Research in advanced manufacturing should be more business led, but this needs to be balanced by consideration of the needs of people in manufacturing.

9. Organisation and people issues have technical implications and these need to be researched.

10. Technologies need to be developed that help to make human skills and judgement more effective and more productive. European Commission research programmes largely ignore this issue.

EXECUTIVE SUMMARY

1. This report contains the results of a study aimed at identifying proposals for future European Commission funded research addressing organisation, people and technology issues in the area of advanced manufacturing. The primary objective of the study was to develop recommendations for research, with emphasis on organisation and people issues and their impact on technological research.

2. A new approach to advanced manufacturing is needed. In the past emphasis has been placed on using technology to reduce costs because competitiveness depended on product price. The markets of the 1990's will be characterised by greater emphasis on product quality and customer choice, and therefore the technology driven strategies that worked so well in the past may not be satisfactory. New approaches are needed, which should be based on organisation, people and technology. This change of approach needs to be incorporated into European Commission funded research programmes.

3. There is a need to adopt a broader approach to manufacturing research. There are many topics that are not at present adequately addressed. Organisation and people issues are one example, manufacturing strategies another. Research also needs to be approached in an interdisciplinary way, because there are many issues that lie between disciplines which need to be considered. The motivation needs of people and the opportunity to make better use of human skills, and the effect that these issues have on technological developments is an example of this kind of interdisciplinary topic.

4. There is a need to undertake awareness activities to increase the understanding of, for example, these organisation and people issues, and the interdisciplinary nature of these topics. Training is also needed to develop a new type of engineer, the Interdisciplinary Manufacturing Systems Engineer. The issues involved in the development of this new breed of engineer need to be researched and appropriate educational and training material and techniques need to be developed. Emphasis should be placed on broadening skills and knowledge as well as training for a life time of learning.

5. There is a need to modify existing research programmes such as ESPRIT-CIM and BRITE-EURAM, and also to establish a new programme to cover any issues that cannot be addressed by existing programmes. There is a need for a more integrated approach within the European Commission towards advanced manufacturing research. Given the importance of manufacturing for the future prosperity of Europe, there is a case for establishing a European Strategic Research Action in Advanced Manufacturing, building on existing programmes and extending the research into new areas.

6. The objectives of this new action should be to: assist European manufacturing industry to become more competitive; modernise the technology, organisation, and work practices used by European manufacturing industry; promote European industrial cooperation in precompetitive advanced manufacturing research; develop an interdisciplinary approach to advanced manufacturing.

7. The research action should address three key themes: advanced manufacturing organisation; advanced manufacturing management and work practices; and advanced manufacturing technology. It should cover a wide range of topics, for example, the organisation of factories, change management techniques, business and manufacturing strategy, interdisciplinary manufacturing systems design, cost accounting techniques, etc.

8. The way forward is to build on what has been achieved thus far. Computer Integrated Manufacturing is important, but needs to be seen as a small part of a broader concept of integration. Industry and the European Commission need to develop a broader understanding of integration. The current emphasis on CIM is misplaced and only serves to focus industry's attention on the wrong issues.

9. There is a consensus on the need for a strategic shift away from automation, especially of decision making, towards using technology to support people. The emphasis needs to be placed on developing skill

supporting rather than skill substituting technologies: technology should be developed which leaves room for the exercise of human skill, judgement and knowledge. Technology should be used to make these distinctive human attributes more productive, and efforts to reproduce these unique characteristics in machines is seen as unproductive, expensive and ultimately futile.

10. It is clear that technologists on their own are unlikely to be able to develop skill supporting technologies. The expertise needed lies outside of engineering. Technologists should therefore collaborate with social scientists and address technology as an interdisciplinary subject.

11. A number of strategic changes are needed. ESPRIT-CIM and BRITE-EURAM should adopt the philosophy underlying that of SPRINT action line 'Specific Projects for Intra-Community Innovation Transfers' which acknowledges that there is a growing need to adopt a global approach, not a purely technical one. Specific projects are therefore expected to employ an overall systems approach, taking into account all the factors necessary to bring about change. These include technological requirements, management and organisation, training and motivation of staff, etc. Projects should be balanced addressing elements of organisation, people and technology.

12. It should be assumed that all projects have an organisation and people dimension. It should be left to proposers to demonstrate that this is not the case. It should therefore be made a condition that proposals identify the organisation and people issues and specify how these will be dealt with. It is important that industrial users give details in proposals of their organisational structures and practices. The information that they should give needs to be clearly specified. Proposers should be expected to justify their organisational structures and procedures. Once a project is running, project monitoring and formal reviews should pay particular attention to the way that organisation and people issues are being addressed by the consortium.

13. Another important issue relevant to submission of project proposals is the business and economic justification of projects. Industrial users should give an explanation of their business plans and explain what cost accounting practices they use. If they are using conventional cost accounting methods, they should explain why they are not using more up-to-date techniques. They should also be asked to give a percentage breakdown of their total manufacturing costs by category (e.g. direct labour, indirect labour, materials, etc.). They should be expected to justify the project with reference to this information.

14. There is scope to undertake a vast amount of research on developing new skill supporting technologies which take into account new organisational concepts, the needs of people and the philosophy of making human skills more productive and more effective. The only constraints on this research are the human imagination, lack of financial support and a shortage of skilled engineers who can work in an interdisciplinary way with social scientist.

15. ESPRIT-CIM and BRITE-EURAM should give consideration to supporting the development of skill supporting technologies. Condition monitoring, free ranging robotic vehicles, database management and networking, applications of genetic algorithms, vision systems, workshop oriented programming of robots and machine tools, decision support systems, computer-aided design, production planning and control systems, etc. are all areas which provide scope for further research with the emphasis on skill supporting technology.

16. Research into technologies that will support a shift in market conditions towards one-of-a-kind production (OKP) should also be considered. The success of OKP depends very much on making use of human intelligence and adaptability and providing the right sort of technology. There is a need therefore to develop technologies that will support this approach to manufacturing.

17. Technologies to support group working are also seen as an important area for future research The increasing emphasis on team or group working demands the development of technologies that will support this method of working. Computer supported cooperative work is therefore an area of research that needs to be considered.

18. Technologies to support the learning company or organisation also need to be developed. This is seen as an important concept for the future.

19. Many people still experience difficulties in accepting that organisation and people issues are primary questions that have an influence on technology. Whilst old ideas cannot be changed overnight, the reluctance to take notice of alternative perspectives is causing frustration and some anger. If existing research programmes are not prepared to fund the interdisciplinary research outlined in this report, then the European Commission should establish a new research programme to fund this research.

ACKNOWLEDGEMENTS

The work of the technical recommendations network (TRN) was made possible by funding provided by the European Commission through the FAST programme and the German State Government of Nordrhein Westfalen through the Nordrhein Westfalen Wissenschaftszentrum Institut Arbeit und Technik.

A large number of people have contributed to the preparation of this report.

I would like to than Dr W. Wobbe of FAST for entrusting the work of the TRN to Cheshire Henbury and for his guidance throughout the course of the project. I would also like to thank Professor Dr F. Lehner, Dr S. von Bandemer, Dr J. Hilbert, Dr.-Ing. P. Brödner, and Dr J. Hennig for many useful and interesting discussions on the issues addressed by the TRN, and for their valuable comments on the first draft of the final report.

The technical recommendations network was made up of the following people:

    Professor J. Browne, University College Galway
    Professor T. Husband, Imperial College, London
    Professor Dr.-Ing. G. Seliger, Technische Universität Berlin
    Professor Dr.-Ing. H.-J. Warnecke, Universität Stuttgart
    Professor G. Doumeingts, University of Bordeaux
    Professor M. Rodd, University of Wales, Swansea
    Professor R. Michelini, Universita di Genova
    Dr I. Sejersen, Dansk Teknologisk Institut
    Dr.ir G. van der Heiden, TNO ITP, Eindhoven
    Dr.-Ing. P. Brödner, Institut Arbeit und Technik
    Dr P. Kidd, Cheshire Henbury

I would like to thank Professors Browne, Husband and Seliger for preparing written contributions for this report. I would also like to thank members of the TRN for participating in the workshop held in April 1990 to discuss the content of the four preliminary papers prepared for the report. I would also like to thank Professor Warnecke for his constructive and helpful comments on the first draft of the final report. Finally, I would also like to thank members of the Commission staff from the ESPRIT-CIM and BRITE-EURAM programmes who provided useful insights into the content and philosophy of these two research programmes.

P.T. Kidd
Macclesfield, November 1990

CONTENTS

KEY ISSUES V

EXECUTIVE SUMMARY VII

ACKNOWLEDGEMENTS XI

INTRODUCTION 1

CHAPTER 1 **ORGANISATION, PEOPLE AND TECHNOLOGY IN ADVANCED MANUFACTURING** 3
   1.1 INTRODUCTION 3
   1.2 ANTHROPOCENTRIC vs. TECHNOCENTRIC 3
      1.2.1 What Does Technocentric Mean? 3
      1.2.2 Anthropocentric: The Opposite of Technocentric? 4
   1.3 ADVANCED MANUFACTURING IN THE 1990's AND BEYOND 5
      1.3.1 The Issues for the 1990's and Beyond 5
      1.3.2 Human Factors or New Manufacturing Strategies? 7
      1.3.3 The Benefits of a Broader and Balanced Approach 8
      1.3.4 Why are People Important? 10
      1.3.5 The Technical Factors of People 10
   1.4 ORGANISATION, PEOPLE AND TECHNOLOGY: THE REFERENCE MODEL FOR THE 1990's AND BEYOND 13

CHAPTER 2 **FUTURE INTEGRATED MANUFACTURING SYSTEMS: A BUSINESS DRIVEN APPROACH** 17
   2.1 INTRODUCTION 17
   2.2 THE MANUFACTURING ENVIRONMENT 17
      2.2.1 Beyond CIM - OKP? 19
      2.2.2 Adaptability and Flexibility 20
      2.2.3 Individuals and Teams 20
   2.3 COMPUTERS IN MANUFACTURING 21
      2.3.1 The Role of Computers in Manufacturing 21
      2.3.2 Production Management Systems 22
      2.3.3 The JIT Approach 24
      2.3.4 JIT Versus MRP 25
      2.3.5 JIT - A Socio-technical Approach? 26
      2.3.6 CAD Systems 27
   2.4 POSSIBLE RESEARCH THEMES 27
      2.4.1 Research Themes on the Design Cycle 28
      2.4.2 The Manufacturing Planning and Control Cycle 28
      2.4.3 The Learning Organisation 29
      2.4.4 The Manufacturing Process 29
   2.5 CONCLUSIONS 29

CHAPTER 3 **ANTHROPOCENTRIC TECHNOLOGIES: THE WAY AHEAD?** 31
   3.1 INTRODUCTION 31
   3.2 BACKGROUND 31
      3.2.1 Human Aspects of AMT 33
      3.2.2 Research into the Design of AMT with a Human Orientation 34
      3.2.3 Relevant Research at Imperial College 35
      3.2.4 ESPRIT Project 1199: Human-Centred CIM 41

3.3 TERMINOLOGY: IS ANTHROPOCENTRIC A HELPFUL LABEL?	42
3.4 COMMERCIAL AND TECHNICAL JUSTIFICATIONS	43
3.4.1 BICC Sealectro	43
3.4.2 Systems Reliability	44
3.4.3 Faster Response and Greater Flexibility	44
3.5 RESEARCH THEMES FOR THE FUTURE	45
3.5.1 Technology	45
3.5.2 Organisation	46
3.5.3 People	47
CHAPTER 4 EUROPEAN RESEARCH IN ADVANCED MANUFACTURING	49
4.1 INTRODUCTION	49
4.2 THE NEW MARKET ENVIRONMENT - THE NEED FOR A CHANGED APPROACH	50
4.2.1 The Problems	50
4.2.2 The Response of the European Commission	51
4.3 THE WAY FORWARD	52
4.3.1 Anthropocentric or Technocentric Research?	53
4.3.2 A New Approach to Technology	55
4.3.3 A Reference Model for Advanced Manufacturing Research in the 1990's	56
4.4 DETAILED PROPOSALS FOR A NEW RESEARCH ACTION	60
4.4.1 Suggested Revisions to the ESPRIT Workprogramme	61
4.4.2 Suggested Revisions to the BRITE-EURAM Workprogramme	63
4.4.3 Examples of Projects	64
CHAPTER 5 MANUFACTURING TECHNOLOGY: AN ANTHROPOCENTRIC APPROACH	67
5.1 INTRODUCTION	67
5.2 A WORKABLE DEFINITION	67
5.3 APPROACH FOR ANTHROPOCENTRIC TECHNOLOGY IN MANUFACTURING	70
5.3.1 Factory Modelling	71
5.3.2 Competence Oriented Workshop Scheduling	74
5.3.3 Rapid Prototyping	75
5.3.4 Expert Systems for Diagnosis	75
5.3.5 Training and Qualification Systems	75
5.3.6 Work Organisation	75
5.3.7 Preservation of Natural Resources	76
5.4 ORGANISATIONAL AND ECONOMIC ASPECTS	77
5.4.1 Zero Reject Production	77
5.4.2 Just-In-Time	77
5.4.3 Qualification as an Asset	77
5.4.4 One of a Kind Production	79
5.4.5 Management	80
5.4.6 Product Properties: Ease of Recycling	80
5.5 COUNTERACTING FORCES	80
5.6 THE SCOPE FOR RESEARCH	81
5.6.1 Factory Modelling	81
5.6.2 Workshop Scheduling	82
5.6.3 Knowledge Based Diagnosis	83
5.6.4 Training and Qualification	84
5.6.5 Work Organisation	84
5.6.6 Recycling of Materials	84
5.7 RESEARCH TOPICS WITH ANTHROPOCENTRIC REFERENCES	84
5.7.1 Factory Modelling	84
5.7.2 Workshop Scheduling	85
5.7.3 Knowledge Based Diagnosis	85
5.7.4 Training and Qualification	85
5.7.5 Work Organisation	86
5.7.6 Recycling	86

CHAPTER 6 **CONCLUSIONS AND RECOMMENDATIONS** 87
    6.1 MAIN CONCLUSIONS 87
    6.2 AN INTEGRATED APPROACH 89
    6.3 AWARENESS 91
    6.4 TRAINING 92
    6.5 ADVANCED MANUFACTURING RESEARCH 93
        6.5.1 Strategic Issues 93
        6.5.2 Specific Research Recommendations 95
        6.5.3 The Next Steps 95
        6.5.4 Final Points 96

REFERENCES 97

INTRODUCTION

This report arises from the work of the Technical Recommendations Network (TRN) of an applied technology assessment study which was concerned with establishing the Perspectives and Conditions for Development of Anthropocentric Production Systems (Commission of the European Communities 1989).

The work was funded by the European Commission programme Forecasting and Assessment in Science and Technology (FAST), and the Government of Nordrhein Westfalen in the Federal Republic of Germany. The prime contractor for the study was the Nordrhein Westfalen Wissenschaftszentrum Institut Arbeit und Technik. The study was organised around three research networks.

The first network, made up of social scientists from each Member State, examined the factors (management, industrial relations, etc.) that might influence the take up and exploitation by industry of Anthropocentric Production Systems. The second network addressed the problem of identifying examples of the industrial application of Anthropocentric Production Systems in the Member States.

The third network was the TRN. The work of the TRN was organised and led by Cheshire Henbury, a research and consultancy company in the UK, with specialist expertise in the area addressed by the study. The objectives of the TRN were to:

. formulate a clear, short and understandable definition of anthropocentric systems;

. define the business and technical reasons why research programmes should address this topic;

. identify the research that needs to be addressed by European Commission research programmes.

The TRN was organised around a number of well known and respected technical experts in manufacturing engineering. These experts were organised into a core group consisting of four people, and an advisory support group consisting of seven people. Members of the core group produced papers that were discussed with members of the advisory support group at a workshop held at the University of Manchester Institute of Science and Technology in April 1990.

Following the discussions with the advisory group at this workshop, the four members of the core group modified their papers. These four modified papers form the basis of this final report of the work of the TRN. The report has been organised along the following lines.

Chapter 1 provides an overview of the issues addressed by the four experts in their papers. These include the business reasons for a new approach to advanced manufacturing and consideration of the basis for this new approach. This section also addresses why organisational change and people are important and provides some insights into the meaning of the term Anthropocentric Production System.

Chapters 2, 3, 4 and 5 consist of the papers produced by the four experts: Professor J Browne, Director of the CIM Research Unit at University College Galway, Professor T Husband, Head of the Department of Mechanical Engineering at the Imperial College of Science and Technology in London, Dr P T Kidd, Director of Cheshire Henbury, and Professor G Seliger from the Institut für Werkzeugmachinen und Fertigungstechnik at the Technische Universität Berlin.

Recommendations for the way forward, including changes to existing European Commission research programmes such as ESPRIT and BRITE-EURAM, the development of new research programmes, and other Community actions, are given Chapter 6.

CHAPTER 1

ORGANISATION, PEOPLE AND TECHNOLOGY

IN

ADVANCED MANUFACTURING

1.1 INTRODUCTION

The aim of this part of the report is to summarise the arguments put forward by the technical experts for an approach to advanced manufacturing based on organisation, people and technology. This chapter therefore sets the scene for the four chapters that follow.

The starting point for this chapter is the term anthropocentric: why is it being used and what are the possible interpretations? This is followed by an explanation of why a new approach to advanced manufacturing is needed. The arguments are related to market factors, and the implications of these market demands are explored. Finally, the analysis leads, not to a definition of the phrase Anthropocentric Production System, but to a statement of the general characteristics of advanced manufacturing systems for the 1990's and beyond.

1.2 ANTHROPOCENTRIC vs. TECHNOCENTRIC

Two issues have stood out during the course of the FAST study. These were the use of the word anthropocentric and the (apparent) problem of making a clear definition of the term. The problem of definition does not arise from any intrinsic difficulties in stating what principles advanced manufacturing systems need to be based on in the 1990's and the early 21st century. These principles are now widely discussed in the literature, for example, in the report prepared by PA Consulting Group for the UK Government's Department of Trade and Industry (DTI 1989a).

The main problem lies in the insistence on using terms which represent over simplified representations of what manufacturing systems are believed to be, i.e. technocentric (meaning technology centred), and what it is believed they should be, i.e. anthropocentric (meaning human centred).

1.2.1 What Does Technocentric Mean?

The design of technocentric systems, it is argued, is dominated by technological considerations. People are treated in a mechanistic way and are regarded as an issue of secondary importance. The worker is seen as a nuisance, a source of uncertainty, a necessary evil. The role of the human is minimised through automation and deskilling, and control over the work is transferred to computers and to management. Technology, on the whole, is viewed as a means of replacing or reducing the role of shop floor people.

The technocentric factory is based on the 1890's model of factory organisation and control illustrated in Figure 1.1 (Kidd 1990a). This involves a factory laid out on a functional or process basis, with turning machines in one part of the factory, milling machines in another part, and so on. Moreover, control of these functions is based on the hub and spoke model, with control and decision making centralised in the planning office. The organisation is very hierarchical, responsibilities are rigidly defined and command and control is exercised from the top downwards.

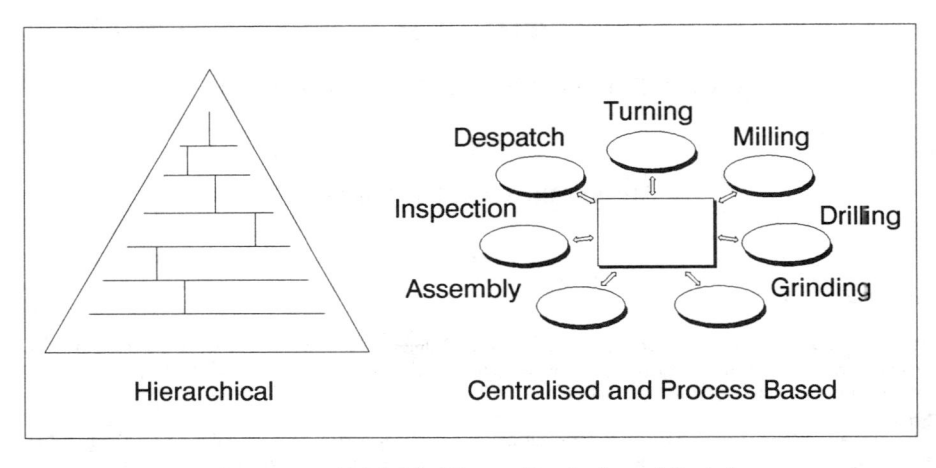

Figure 1.1: 1890's Model of Factory Organisation and Control

One notable person involved in the development of factory management techniques in the late 19th century, and often criticised today, was Frederick Taylor. Taylor's system of factory management is based on the belief that workers need to be told exactly what to do. Taylor also believed that working methods should be standardised and that there was only one best way of doing work, which could be scientifically established. Functional specialisation and work simplification are needed, and decision making should be taken away from the workers and centralised in a factory planning office (Taylor 1902, 1907).

Taylor is often vilified as the archetypal engineer: technocentric in nature, narrow in outlook, and unconcerned with the human implications of his beliefs and actions.

1.2.2 Anthropocentric: The Opposite of Technocentric?

Anthropocentric systems sometimes seem to be viewed as the opposite to the Tayloristic and technocentric philosophy in almost every respect.

Whilst there is some truth in the technocentric characterisation of manufacturing industry, it is of course a gross caricature of the real situation and such a gross over simplification is not very helpful. It does not adequately represent the complexity of manufacturing.

The term anthropocentric has primarily served as a focus of concern about the technology led development of advanced manufacturing during the 1980's and the retention of the organisational structures and work practices that were developed in the late 19th century. It has also served as a counterbalance to the rational model of human behaviour and the mechanistic way that people are treated by some managers and technologists.

It is also the case that there are those who are suggesting that anthropocentric systems are the exact opposite and the alternative to so called technocentric systems. Such an understanding however is based on a black and white analysis. In effect they are suggesting that there are only two options, technocentric and anthropocentric, and that there is nothing in between, no meeting point, no compromise.

Anthropocentric, viewed in this sense, is Taylorism in reverse. It displays the same lack of balance and realism that Taylor himself showed when trying to spread his own ideas (which incidentally were never implemented in full because of the extremity and human implications of what he was proposing). It is another prescriptive solution and industry does not need prescriptive solutions.

The term Anthropocentric, therefore, seems to be used in a number of ways. The first is legitimate and is as a counterbalance to the extremes of the so called technocentric view. The second is as an extreme alternative which lacks balance and which is as prescriptive as the so called technocentric approach.

1.3 ADVANCED MANUFACTURING IN THE 1990's AND BEYOND

The real issue is not whether Industry and the European Commission should adopt anthropocentric either as a label or as an alternative to the so called technocentric philosophy. It is more a question of what Industry and the European Commission should do to change to a perspective that is more balanced and which is more in tune with Industry's needs. To do this it is necessary, as Bolk (1989, 1990) has attempted to do at two ESPRIT CIM-Europe conferences, to map out the new management and organisational perspective within which research programmes such as ESPRIT-CIM and BRITE-EURAM can find a new focus.

1.3.1 The Issues for the 1990's and Beyond

There is an every growing body of people who believe that human competence will play an important role in future manufacturing systems. There are numerous reasons for this belief, but they are primarily related to market conditions.

World markets are becoming more dynamic and customer driven, and competition on price alone is no longer a viable business strategy for most manufacturing companies. Other non-price competitive factors have become more important.

During the 1990's there will also be an increasing trend towards tailoring of products to meet customer needs. Although this trend has been described as a move from mass production to one of a kind production, the actual change in market conditions is more complex than this because there are a whole range of company specific conditions governing strategic choice (Atkinson 1990). A more realistic, yet still simplified representation of the changes that are now occurring, is illustrated in Figure 1.2. Basically the emphasis is on moving from price competition to quality competition. This can be based on large batches of specialised brand products or low batches of diversified quality products.

	Price Competition	Quality Competition
Large Batch Production	MASS PRODUCTION 1	SPECIALISED BRAND PRODUCTION 2
Small Batch Production	3 COMPONENT SUB CONTRACTING	4 DIVERSIFIED QUALITY PRODUCTION

Figure 1.2: Simplified Classification of Business Strategies (Source: Atkinson 1990)

These changes in business strategies do not mean that price competition is dead. In fact there is the opportunity for the most innovative companies to offer a diverse range of low price high quality products.

The important point about these changes in markets is that they have led to the trends depicted in Figure 1.3: reductions in production volumes, increased product variety, shorter product life cycles (as companies strive to keep their products up to date), and a reduced number of repeat orders. These trends are set to continue throughout the 1990's. Opportunities for profit growth will not therefore be derived from economies of scale, but from economies of scope, i.e. competitive advantage will be derived from flexibility rather than from low costs (Williamson 1989). The key business issues are therefore to reduce manufacturing lead time (including product development time), improve customer service, reduce inventory and increase responsiveness, against a background of highly variable customer demand patterns and changing specifications (Hamlin 1989a).

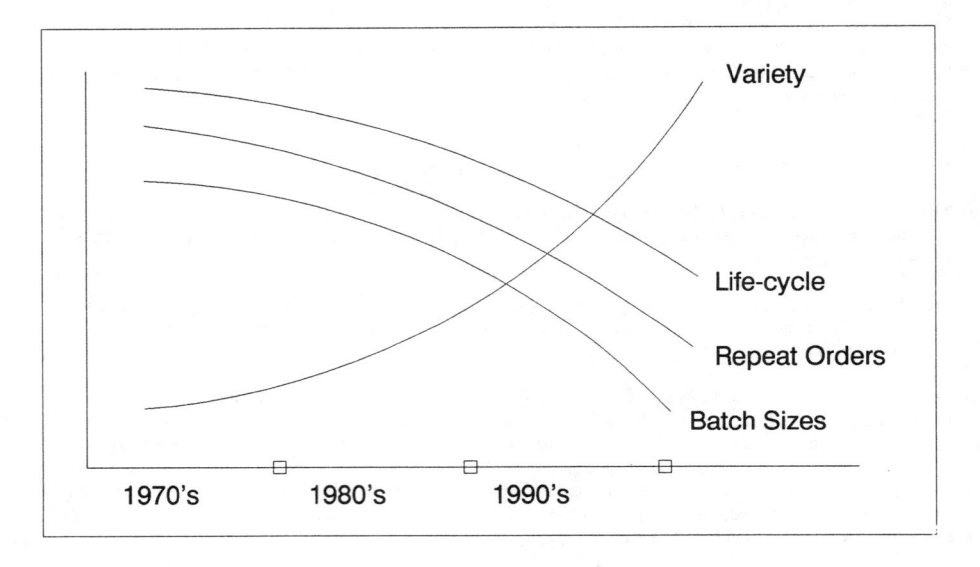

Figure 1.3: Market Trends

European manufacturing companies will therefore in general, have to achieve, without compromise, three potentially conflicting goals: reduced costs, improved quality and greater flexibility. This however is only part of the story. Improved competitiveness once achieved has to be retained. This will be achieved by companies transforming themselves into learning organisations seeking continuing improvement in every aspect of their activities (Hayes, Wheelwright and Clark 1988).

Hayes, Wheelwright and Clark (1988) have argued that it is not often fully understood that a company's competitive position at any point in time is less important than the rate of improvement as compared with its competitors. Manufacturing competitiveness is not static. There is no project, no investment, that will provide the magic solution to lack of competitiveness. Manufacturing competitiveness is a dynamic process, and to remain competitive it is necessary for companies to become learning organisations seeking continuing improvement in everything that they do.

Here is the crucial point. None of these goals cannot be achieved using technology alone. Technology is not even the most important factor. It is important, no company will be able to compete without making use of technology, but organisation and people are equally important. There is no single element that should be given priority. A broad approach is needed that is based on organisation, people and technology.

1.3.2 Human Factors or New Manufacturing Strategies?

The change that industry needs to make in its approach is illustrated in Figure 1.4. Over the past ten years Computer Integrated Manufacturing (CIM) has been one of the major research areas funded by the European Commission and Industry. Much of the work on CIM has been dominated by technological considerations. The concept of integrated manufacturing should not however be restricted to computers, data interchange, standards, and software modules. This is only part of the story.

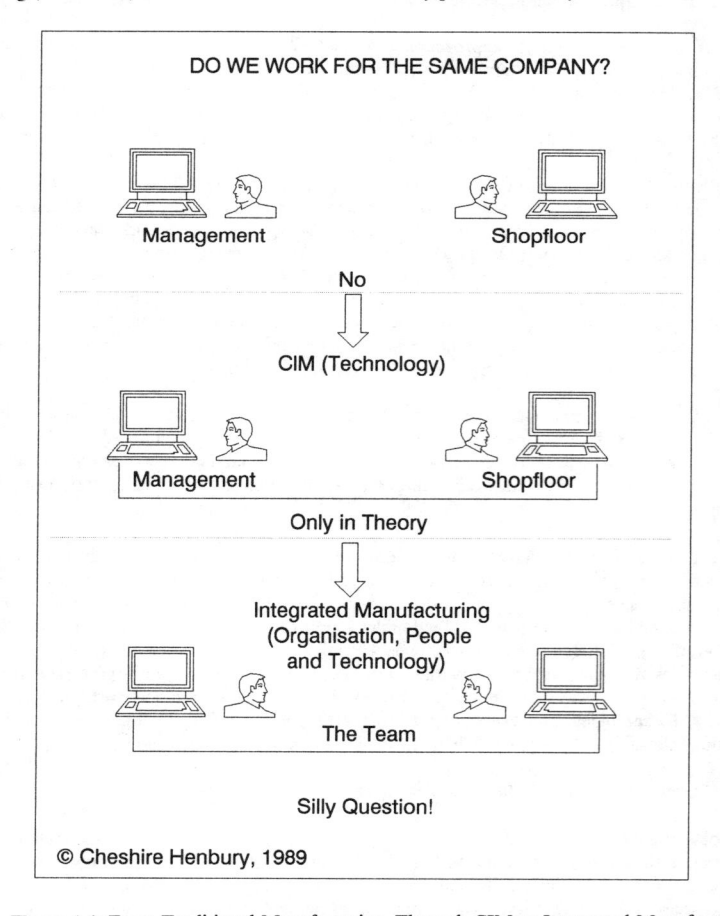

```
┌─────────────────────────────────────────────┐
│         DO WE WORK FOR THE SAME COMPANY?    │
│                                             │
│     [PC] [person]         [person] [PC]     │
│      Management            Shopfloor        │
│                                             │
│                    No                       │
│                    ⇩                        │
│              CIM (Technology)               │
│                                             │
│     [PC] [person]         [person] [PC]     │
│      Management            Shopfloor        │
│                                             │
│                Only in Theory               │
│                    ⇩                        │
│            Integrated Manufacturing         │
│             (Organisation, People           │
│                and Technology)              │
│                                             │
│     [PC] [person]─────────[person] [PC]     │
│                   The Team                  │
│                                             │
│                Silly Question!              │
│                                             │
│  © Cheshire Henbury, 1989                   │
└─────────────────────────────────────────────┘
```

Figure 1.4: From Traditional Manufacturing, Through CIM to Integrated Manufacturing

The Oxford English dictionary definition of integrate is "to combine parts into a whole". An integrated manufacturing (IM) system cannot be achieved by just linking computers together, sharing data, and attempting to automate various tasks. Integration implies cooperation and coordination. The whole implies more than just linking computers and coordinating tasks such as design and manufacturing. It is more than technology. It includes people, working practices, organisational structure as well as technology. No amount of technology can make people cooperate, and people will have to cooperate, because it is only through cooperation that integrated manufacturing will be achieved.

Achieving integrated manufacturing therefore needs more than just technology. It also needs changes in attitude, work practices and organisation. But this is not just about changing organisations and work practices to fit the computer interfaced technology. This is only one issue. Organisation and people can actually provide solutions to manufacturing problems and can lead to improved competitiveness. In essence the organisation and people issues are not just a question of human factors in manufacturing, but are more a question of developing manufacturing strategies that specifically set out to use organisation, people and technology to achieve improved competitiveness.

The differences between these two approaches are fundamental. Human factors in manufacturing traditionally has been concerned with improving working conditions, or with making equipment easier to use, or with smoothing the introduction of new technologies, or all three. It does not however question whether the technology is appropriate. The technology remains fixed. Human factors specialists will design the interfaces to the technology and design the work practices and jobs around the given technology.

This approach is used for a number of reasons. First, many human factors people do not fully understand the technology. Second, many of them do not fully appreciate the interdisciplinary issues. For example, if the organisational structure emphasises decentralised control around product based manufacturing cells, then the technology needed in this situation is quite different from the case where control is centralised. At best human factors specialists adopt a multidisciplinary approach. Third, they largely ignore the impact that organisational change and new work practices can have on business performance. They may argue that joint optimisation of human and technical design issues will avoid implementation problems and result in more effective systems because human needs are taken into account, but they do not seem to understand that organisational choice and the role of people can be used to satisfy business needs.

It should be added that engineers, while understanding the technology, often have much the same understanding of the role of human factors and the associated design issues. It may be that this traditional human factors method is what industry is looking for. Business as usual, i.e. technology is the answer, but this time with a human touch. If this is so then they will find the human factors field offers just what they are looking for.

They will however miss the opportunity to adopt a more sensible and balanced approach that seeks to use organisation, people and technology as the three basic components of a manufacturing strategy that will satisfy the business needs of a company. Instead of just looking to technology to provide improved competitiveness, manufacturing companies should address how these three elements can produce business benefits. Instead of looking for prescriptive solutions, which is often what technology offers, manufacturing companies should design appropriate organisations and work practices, define an appropriate role for people, and then use technology in a way that reflects the needs of the new organisation and work practices. Instead of installing new technologies, and then adapting the organisation and the people to the technology, companies should consider adapting the technology to the organisation and the people.

1.3.3 The Benefits of a Broader and Balanced Approach

The benefits of a manufacturing strategy based on organisation, people and technology include: shorter throughput times, reduced inventory, improved product quality, more economic operating conditions, and improved responsiveness. For example, by changing the factory to a product based organisational structure it is possible to shorten throughput times by as much as 80 percent and to reduce in-process inventory by as much as 60 percent (Brödner 1984). The key point is that these benefits can be achieved without any investment in new technology. These are the results of organisational changes. These changes can also result in simplified material flows, easier production planning and control, and improved job satisfaction which can lead to more highly motivated people.

In Germany one company (see Klingenberg and Kranzle 1987) reorganised its factory from a traditional process layout to a product based organisation. The claimed improvements are shown in Figure 1.5. The organisational changes led to a 10 percent increase in direct labour costs because the role of shop floor employees was expanded, but indirect labour costs have been significantly reduced.

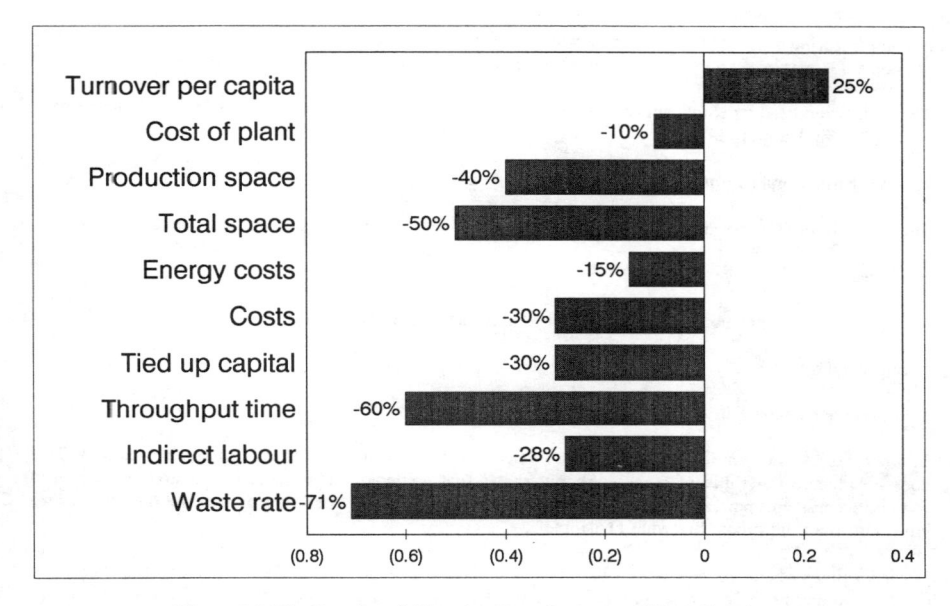

Metric	Value
Turnover per capita	25%
Cost of plant	-10%
Production space	-40%
Total space	-50%
Energy costs	-15%
Costs	-30%
Tied up capital	-30%
Throughput time	-60%
Indirect labour	-28%
Waste rate	-71%

Figure 1.5: The Benefits of Changing Organisation and Work Practices

As a result of these organisational and work practice changes the company has achieved: improved due date performance, a high speed of response to quantitative and qualitative changes of demand, improved quality, reduced expenditure on computer equipment, and a reduction in breakdowns.

Costs have been reduced because there has been a net reduction in labour and because less capital is needed to fund the business. Improvements in quality arise because shop floor employees are now responsible for the quality of their work. Defects can therefore be detected at an earlier stage or can be avoided altogether. This brings further cost savings through reduced rework and scrap.

Improvements in flexibility have been achieved because throughput times have been reduced. Organisational factors which lengthen throughput times include too many levels in the hierarchy, too many functional departments, complex procedures and long signal processing times. Organisational changes that lead to reduced hierarchies, a smaller number of departments, simpler procedures and faster signal processing can therefore result in shorter throughput times.

The factory planning and control functions can also become much simpler as a result of organisational changes. Systems are no longer needed which attempt to organise the correct schedule of work for every single operation on every single resource at every moment of time. Instead the system only needs to provide the factory planner with information allowing each product based manufacturing cell to be loaded with a sensible volume of work over a period of time. The detailed planning and scheduling can be done by the shop floor employees working in the cells. This results in effective but simpler and cheaper computer systems.

Organisational changes can also provide the basis for achieving continuing improvement in manufacturing. For example, a rejected part, or a half finished item waiting for new tooling, or a part program that can be improved, or a design feature that leads to machining difficulties, represent time and money that is being wasted and competitive opportunities missed. Remedying these problems is what continuing improvement in manufacturing is about. This is an issue which concerns shop floor employees, but to tap into the creativity of shop floor employees new organisational structures and new work practices are needed.

The results reported by Klingenberg and Kranzle (1987) are not an isolated example. Similar benefits have been noted by Hamlin (1989b).

1.3.4 Why are People Important?

The example used above demonstrates that organisational change is important because it can lead to:

- reduced costs;

- reduced throughput times hence greater flexibility and responsiveness;

- improved quality;

- support for continuing improvement.

In other words non technical solutions can be found to the problems faced by manufacturing industry. This does not negate the value of technology, but shows that technology is not the sole source of improved competitiveness and performance. So organisation and technology are both important, and one is no more important than the other. But what of people?

In earlier times when competition was based on price, cost was the most important consideration. To remain competitive and profitable, costs had to be continually reduced and, as labour was a major cost, it was not unnatural to regard people on the shop floor as a cost to be minimised. This is largely why there has been a tendency to use technology to replace people.

Because direct labour costs are now often only a small percentage of total manufacturing costs, and in the light of market factors discussed earlier, the traditional cost driven approach no longer makes any sense. People on the shop floor are not now a cost - they are a resource. Their skills and experience are needed, not just to compensate for the limitations of the technology or to do the tasks that cannot be automated, but primarily:

- to complement the organisation and the technology;

- to provide flexibility and adaptation;

- to provide continuing improvement in products and processes;

- to contribute their unique abilities and skills.

In essence, the competence of shop floor people is now a requirement for competitive manufacturing. Previously it has been seen as a hindrance. The essence of a new approach to manufacturing lies in securing and unleashing the skills and talents of the shop floor employees. This however is a challenging task and one that not only needs a change in beliefs, but also a change in design practice.

1.3.5 The Technical Factors of People

The change of emphasis from people as a cost to people as a resource has implications for technology. These implications were seen as far back as the early 1960's (Jordan 1963).

It has been customary to design machines (especially those destined for use on the shop floor) as automated systems. Normally, those tasks that cannot be automated for technical and economic reason are left to people to perform (Bainbridge 1983). People are viewed by the designers as a link in the system and have consequently been given only the information and means to do the job assigned as a link. When the system breaks down a person in a link position is as helpless as any other machine component in the system. The possibility of using the system in a way that allows people to take over in an effective way has been designed out.

The literature on human factors is full of papers addressing a topic called allocation of functions between people and machines, which basically means methods for deciding what the machine should do and what people should do. Jordan (1963) says that allocation of functions methods are based on a belief that people and machines are comparable. Basically, humans are flexible but are not consistent whereas machines are consistent but not flexible. Jordan, however, says that this concept of comparability is wrong and that in fact people and machines are complementary. So rather than trying to compare human and machine and deciding which is better at doing a particular task and then designing the technology on this basis, the design problem is one of thinking how people can be complemented by machines and vice versa.

Jordan then states that this line of thought leads to the conclusion that the term allocation of functions between people and machines is meaningless. Rather the issue is one of thinking about how a task can be done by people and machines.

This idea seems largely to have been ignored, except by one engineer (see Rosenbrock 1989), who in the early 1980's, arriving independently at the same conclusions, started to pursue its technological implications. It turns out that the idea provides a possible solution to a major problem posed by new technology: motivation of people.

In Jordan's paper the point is made that when designing a machine the physical environment is always taken into account (i.e. its power supply, its maintenance requirements, the physical setting in which it operates, etc.). The physical environment of a human being is also taken into account, to a greater or lessor extent (i.e. illumination, ventilation, noise levels, human machine interface characteristics, working hours, etc.). However, a fundamental difference between people and machines is that people also have a psychological environment for which an adequate physical environment is a necessary condition but is ultimately secondary in importance.

The psychological environment is subsumed under one word: motivation. The problems of human motivation have been largely ignored, not only by the technical community but also by the human factors community, at least in respect to the design of technology.

Unless people are motivated they will not function as a complement to machines, and the motivation to function as a complement must be considered as a criteria when designing the technology. Unless the work represents a challenge to the users, they will not use their flexibility, their experience, their skills and their judgement. They will not learn nor will they assume responsibility. By designing technology for people to do the least, all challenge is eliminated from the job. Challenge must therefore be built into the technology, otherwise people will just begin to function like a machine.

An important concluding point to this line of argument is that here too people differ significantly from machines. When people are forced to function like a machine they sense that they are being used inefficiently and considered as stupid. People cannot tolerate being used in this way. Overtly or covertly they resist and rebel against it. Nothing could be more inefficient and self-defeating in the long term than to design technology which causes the people who will have to use it to rebel against it.

Jordan closes his paper by stating that herein lies the future challenge to the human factors community. The challenge has never been taken up by these people. It has in fact taken a group of engineers to recognise the wisdom of Jordan's arguments.

The need to consider people and motivation when designing new technologies for the shop floor is likely to become a major problem in the years ahead. It has been argued only recently that there is a need to overcome the Victorian Hell Hole image of manufacturing if more people are to be attracted to work on the shop floor (Dempsey 1990). In the same paper it is also argued that the shortage of skilled people will mean that more automation will be needed on the shop floor.

On the one hand there is a desire to motivate people, to introduce greater flexibility, to manage change, and to make better use of people. Yet there still persists a belief that technology can be introduced as a substitute for human skills, without having damaging consequences for motivation.

This is not an argument against skill substituting technologies or automation. The major issue here is one of motivation and the question of user acceptance and the useability of new technologies. If industry wants to tap into the creativity of shop floor people, to make better use of their skills, then these questions cannot be ignored by those who design new technologies.

Too often the normal procedure when designing new technology is not to take any account of the end user's methods of working, existing skills or personal feelings. Typically, new products start life in research laboratories and arrive on the shop floor demanding new working methods and new skills. This can be compared with trying to fit square pegs into round holes as illustrated in Figure 1.6 (Kidd 1991a).

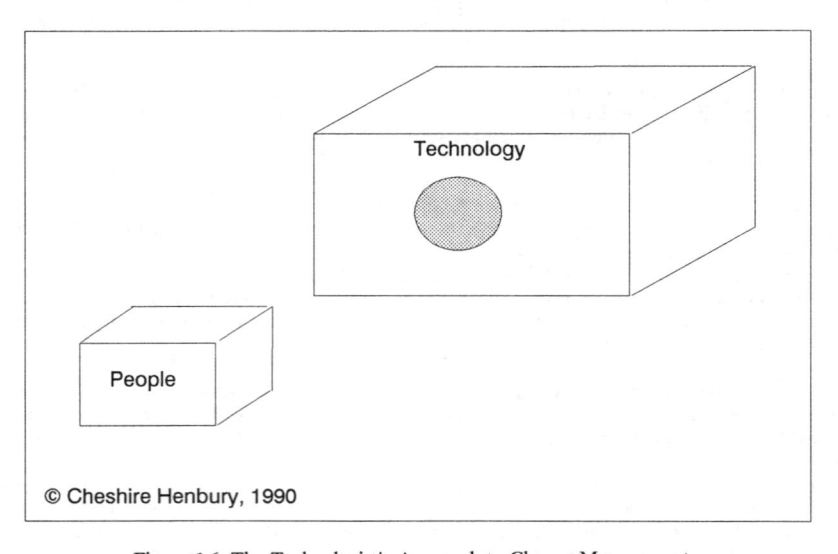

Figure 1.6: The Technologist's Approach to Change Management

Whilst there is nothing wrong with new working methods and new skills, some account should be taken of existing skills and working methods, for the simple reason that it is more likely that new technology will be accepted if it provides some familiar starting point for the end user. This is especially true for older workers who sometimes find accepting new technology a more difficult process than younger people do. With the falling number of school leavers, industry is going to have to rely more on older workers, and the needs of these people will have to be taken into account if lack of motivation and resistance to change are to be avoided.

Industry and the European Commission therefore not only need to understand that the issues are about using organisation, people and technology to satisfy business needs and to improve competitiveness, but that there is a need to address the technical factors of people. In short, technology should be designed using organisational and psychological concepts as well as technical and economic ones.

1.4 ORGANISATION, PEOPLE AND TECHNOLOGY: THE REFERENCE MODEL FOR THE 1990's AND BEYOND

Organisation, people and technology will form the basis of advanced manufacturing in the 1990's and beyond. Technology alone will not provide improved competitiveness. Human competence will play an important role in advanced manufacturing, and research programmes such as ESPRIT and BRITE-EURAM need a new focus to reflect this.

What is needed is an underlying principle that can be used to shape new research programmes. The requirement for flexibility, adaptation, improved responsiveness, and the need to motivate people and to make use of their skills, judgement and experience, all suggest that organisations, work practices and technology need to be developed in a way that will allow highly trained people, at all levels in the company, to adapt their work strategies to the variety of situations that they will have to face. This implies that organisation, work practices and technology will have to be developed as open systems.

An open system allows people a large degree of freedom to define the mode of operation of the system and the form of interaction with the system and its environment. The term implies a system which is flexible. At the moment the term is very much associated in manufacturing with system architectures based on the International Standards Organisation Open Systems Interconnection (ISO-OSI) model. The concept of an open system is also used in management science however, to describe an organisational structure that takes into account and responds to the environment. The idea can however be given a much broader interpretation. It can be applied not only to system architectures and organisational structures, but also to work practices, human-computer interfaces and the relationship between system users and technologies such as shop floor scheduling and control systems, decision support systems, etc. (Kidd 1990b, 1990c, 1991b).

New management perspectives are needed in industry. One possibility is what Peters and Waterman (1982) have termed the open system, social actor approach, which recognises the social and open nature of organisations. In other words, the organisation must take into account and respond to the environment (open systems) and decisions must be taken on the basis of the dynamics that affect people working in groups (social actor).

There is a need to create a new organisational model that will not only be effective and responsive, but will take into account peoples need for motivation. This 1990's model of the organisation is shown in Figure 1.7 (Kidd 1990a). It is based on:

. a flat organisational hierarchy;

. a cell-based factory;

. decentralisation of decision making and control;

. increased competence of shop floor people;

. multiskilled employees;

. team working;

. empowering of people on the shop floor;

. skill supporting technologies;

. continuing improvement involving all employees.

It is necessary here to stress that this is not a prescriptive framework for research in the area of advanced manufacturing, nor is it intended to be a prescriptive solution to the various problems that beset manufacturing industry. The needs of manufacturing industry are not amenable to prescriptive solutions. The

PA Consulting Group's report, Manufacturing into the late 1990's (DTI 1989a), makes a point regarding the different integration needs of manufacturing business. This point is applicable to all aspects of manufacturing systems design:

".... one of the difficulties is that there are so many different types of manufacturing business; high volume and low variety, low volume and high variety, process, batch and jobbing, long and short life cycles, and all these businesses are trying to differentiate in different ways and to compete in a wide range of markets. This of course means that there are a very wide range of critical competences for each type of business ...."

The preceding list should therefore be considered as a general reference model that provides a guide to the development of research programmes, projects and the design of advanced manufacturing systems.

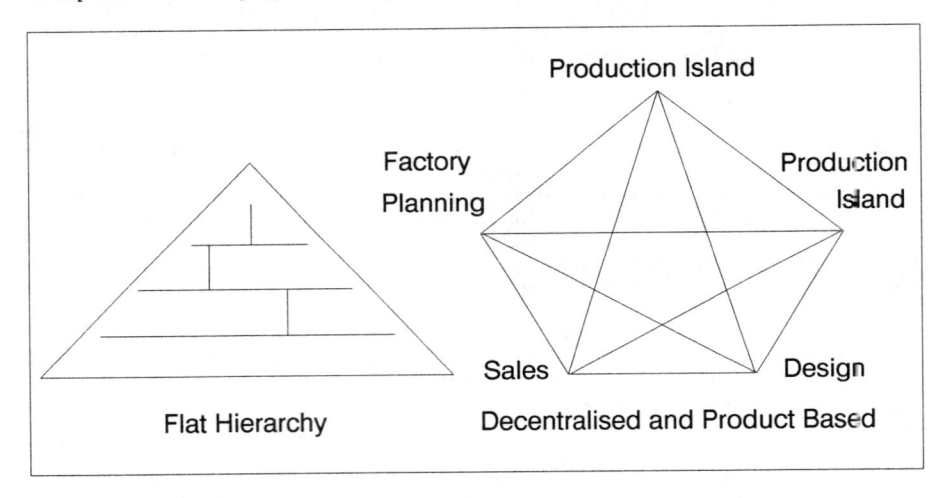

Figure 1.7: 1990's Model of Factory Organisation and Control

It is also necessary to stress that this list of characteristics is not unique to those who advocate an anthropocentric approach. They can also be found in the PA Consulting Group report already referred to, and else where (e.g. Hayes Wheelwright and Clark 1988). It must not be thought either that skill supporting technologies are unique to those who use the anthropocentric label. PA point out in their report that:

"Increasing capital/labour ratios will heighten companies' dependence on the critical skills vital to successful use of new technologies. The more effective responses will include specifying and choosing new technologies that fit well with the current/potential human and organisational capabilities of the company .... analysing carefully the future workforce requirements of new technologies ...."

This points to the need for research and technological design in advanced manufacturing to be based on an interdisciplinary approach. At the moment advanced manufacturing is imbalanced, too much attention is paid to technology, and is largely multidisciplinary. Research also needs to be more business led, and organisation and people should not be treated as issues of secondary importance. The technology should be designed to take account of organisation and people considerations.

What is needed in the sphere of technological development is a new relationship between user and computer: an intelligent relationship between computers and intelligent people.

It has already been mentioned that traditional thinking is often based on the view that the user's role is to compensate for the inadequacies of the computer. The implications of this is that people have to intervene in the system operation. People are still needed.

Research programmes should now focus more on the principle that the user's role is not just to intervene but to be involved. This demands that people be viewed as desirable; the emphasis is therefore upon the phrase 'should be needed', rather than the phrase 'still needed'.

The difference between these two design perspectives is important and needs to be clearly understood. The former views people as complementary to the technology, the latter regards people as a necessity. The first encompasses the second, but not visa versa (Kidd 1988, 1989, 1990d).

The aim should not be to fossilise outdated techniques, but to:

. ease the transition from old to new working methods;

. create a flexible system which will allow skilled users to develop working methods that are appropriate to each situation;

. leave room for users to develop and practice their skills and to contribute their skills, experience and judgement to the work process.

Technical functionality should not therefore be king. User acceptance, useability, user motivation, and other user needs should play an important part in future development of technology.

CHAPTER 2

FUTURE INTEGRATED MANUFACTURING SYSTEMS:

A BUSINESS DRIVEN APPROACH

by

Professor J Browne

CIM Research Unit
University College
Galway
Republic of Ireland

2.1 INTRODUCTION

This chapter explores the background to the development of advanced manufacturing systems. It argues that the modern manufacturing environment is placing tremendous pressures on the manufacturing enterprise in terms of the its ability to supply 'customised' products, with very short delivery times, to a mass market.

The trend is towards One of a Kind Production (OKP). OKP requires flexible and adaptable manufacturing systems. Flexibility can be offered through technology. However adaptability, which implies the ability to respond to an uncertain environment, requires intelligence. Since *intelligence* is the prerogative of human kind, it follows that the OKP system must be designed around the creative abilities of humans. Further, within an OKP environment the need for short turnaround times in design and manufacturing implies that individuals from different departments and disciplines must work together to respond quickly to customer demands. Thus work systems must be developed which support group activity, and technology is needed which enhances group work activity, as well as individual creativity.

The structure of this paper is as follows. First, the modern manufacturing environment is reviewed (section 2.2) and arguments that OKP represents the logical outcome of present trends are presented (section 2.2.1). A distinction between adaptability and flexibility is then made (section 2.2.2) and it is argued that OKP needs adaptability and effective team working (section 2.2.3).

Section 2.3 examines the various roles that computers play in manufacturing today. In particular two well known application areas, Production Management Systems and Computer Aided Design (CAD) are described. The experience of these application areas and the reasons for the failure to realise the potential benefits of these approaches is discussed. It is argued that frequently, failure is caused by the technology driven approaches of the developers and installers of such systems. Materials Requirements Planning (MRP) and Just In Time (JIT) approaches are contrasted. It is argued that JIT is holistic and partially socio-technical (see sections 2.3.3, 2.3.4 and 2.3.5).

Research themes are identified in section 2.4, and in section 2.5 some conclusions are drawn on the need to adapt a skill enhancing approach to the development of technology to be used in an OKP environment.

2.2 THE MANUFACTURING ENVIRONMENT

Today's manufacturing environment is extremely complex and subject to great change. In particular it should be noted that:

- Product variety has greatly increased - mass production is history;

- Product life cycles are often measured in months - not years;

- Cost patterns, particularly in terms of the ratio of material and overhead to labour costs have greatly changed.

Moreover, consumers have tremendous expectations in terms of product quality, delivery lead times and value for money.

Manufacturing systems engineers are trying to design and operate manufacturing systems which facilitate **flexibility**, shorter **design cycle time**, reduced **time to market** for new products, and shorter **order cycle time** to the customer for existing products. Each of these factors will now be briefly discussed.

Increased Product Diversity

The market is no longer satisfied with a mass produced uniform product. Manufacturing firms must now compete by offering variety. The age of the **personalised** consumer product seems to be rapidly approaching. This represents a much changed situation from earlier in this century. The explosion of product variety is particularly evident in the automobile and computer industries. However product variety dramatically increases the complexity of the tasks of process design and production management. For instance, frequent process change-over can be a significant burden. Offering increased choice at reduced cost thus poses significant challenges for the manufacturing firm that is attempting to achieve or maintain competitiveness.

Greatly Reduced Product Life Cycles

The life cycle of a product falls naturally into several phases. In simple terms these are the design phase, the manufacturing phase and the end-of-life phase. Demand is light and grows very slowly in the initial periods, during which the manufacturer can establish the product design and production method. The second stage is one of a mature product enjoying high stable demand. The third and final stage sees the gradual decline in demand for the product. The costs incurred during the early part of the design cycle include the design costs and the costs associated with developing and installing the production process.

In the old way of doing business, the design cycle and the manufacturing cycle were separated and occurred *sequentially*. A product design was proven before it entered production. There was thus a significant amount of time available for production methods to be established prior to volume production of the product. Once the product was established in the market place, the manufacturer could look forward to a relatively high demand for a number of years before the product became obsolete. The many years of high, stable demand enabled the costs incurred in the early stage of product and process development to be recovered.

The difficulty in today's manufacturing environment is that manufacturing can no longer look forward to many years of stable high demand. This is because product re-design is a continuing process, and a product's useful life in the market place is constantly under attack from improved versions incorporating the latest design features. Moreover, firms must strive to get their products to the market place in ever shortening times. All of this means that manufacturing must put processes in place which are sufficiently flexible to accommodate new product designs rapidly without incurring large process introduction costs. Otherwise the costs incurred in the product design and process development phase will be too large to be recovered over the much shorter peak demand phase of the product life cycle.

Because of the compression of product life cycles, manufacturing firms can no longer expend huge resources on developing a dedicated production capability, since the product design is likely to change before that production facility has been paid for. The concept of **economies of scale** have been replaced by the notion of **economies of scope**.

Goldhar et al. (1985) explains that economies of scope exist "when the same equipment can produce multiple products more cheaply in combination than separately. A computer controlled machine does not care whether it works in succession on a dozen different product designs - within, of course, a family of design limits. Change-over times (and therefore costs) are negligible, since the task of machine set-up involves little more than reading a computer program". Moreover, this has implications for investment appraisal procedures since companies must now put in place flexible production facilities which will be used not only on existing product designs but also on future re-designs of these products. In summary, the combination of greater product diversity, shorter product life cycles and pressures for faster time to market have given rise to the need for economies of scope.

Changing Cost Structures

Traditionally manufacturing costs have fallen under three headings, Material Cost, Labour Cost and Overhead. Moreover, labour hours were used in many industries as a base for *recovering* overhead. Bonsack (1986) points out that "current overhead accounting most often uses the **full absorption** method which assigns all factory overhead to units of production based on the labour costs incurred". What happens when direct labour costs reduce to a very small fraction of total cost, to below five percent as is the case in very many factories today?

A number of important characteristics of this new emerging competitive environment have now been identified. This environment has significant implications for the manner in which industrial firms organise their manufacturing processes and procedures. In effect manufacturing is moving into an era of customised products and in fact has come full circle. Manufacturing started with craftsmen producing one-off customised products for a very small market (i.e. the lords etc. who could afford their products). Once again it is necessary to supply *customised products*, but this time with very short delivery lead times to a *mass market*.

2.2.1 Beyond CIM - OKP?

Today CIM factories are regarded as state of the art manufacturing. CIM supports a certain level of variety. It will not support complete customisation. The next stage in manufacturing is OKP (One of a Kind Production).

Year	Manufacturing	
		Standardisation
1920	Mass Production	
1970	FMS	↓
1980	CIM Systems	
2000?	One-of-a-kind Production	Customisation

Figure 2.1: Trends in Manufacturing Systems

Shipbuilding is OKP. Maybe it is possible to learn from the shipbuilders and the aircraft manufacturers? The complexity of these industries is well known, but their customers are happy with lead times measured in months!

Living in an OKP world is only possible with a truly *responsive manufacturing system* - a system which is capable of talking to a customer, 're-engineering' the product to meet his needs, working out how to produce it and finally organising the manufacturing plant to get it completed and out to the customer in hours and days. Also do this regularly and at a cost which makes the product affordable for the customer.

This level of responsiveness cannot be delivered by technology. **Technology is necessary but not sufficient.** Technology can provide the basic infrastructure upon which this responsiveness can be built. However, before developing this argument any further, the role that technology (meaning in this context computer technology) plays in manufacturing systems should be examined, because it can be shown that technology has not really succeeded in satisfying the need for flexibility and adaptability.

2.2.2 Adaptability and Flexibility

Up to now the emphasis has been placed on the development of the technical infrastructure to support automation and to realise CIM. We are inundated with programmes such as Design to Build, MRP II, Statistical Process Control etc. To compete in today's complex environment a firm must also develop it's non technical or social infrastructure; i.e. the skills of its people, the organisational structure within which they operate, the mechanisms they use to realise particular tasks, in particular those tasks which require groups of people to work together to achieve a common task. Organisational structures must be developed which accommodate more *interactive and co-operative working relationships*. Management must cultivate new skills and managerial styles. Companies must be willing to invest as much in the social infrastructure as they have in the technical base.

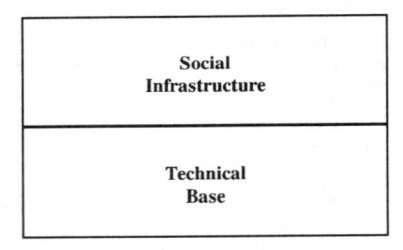

Figure 2.2: Social Infrastructure

In short companies must seek to realise **flexible** and **adaptable** manufacturing systems. **Flexibility is a product of the underlying technology, while adaptability, which implies intelligence is a product of the people in the manufacturing system using the technology to best advantage.**

Further it must be understood that, increasingly, success depends on supporting teams of interdisciplinary workers in the performance of relatively unstructured or reasonably novel tasks - constant redesign of product, changing process technology etc. However up to now the technologists have concentrated on the individual worker, providing for example engineering workstations to support the individual engineer in the performance of some of his work.

2.2.3 Individuals and Teams

Frequently solutions to a problem are sought in terms of finding the right expertise to tackle and solve it. This normally means looking to individuals and providing them with the tools to do the job. In fact much of technology is designed to be used by the expert individual. Workstations are the classic example. Engineers and AI experts are offered powerful workstations and associated software. But in the OKP world success will depend more on the ability of multiskilled teams to work together to address large **problems** as distinct from the **puzzles** which are tackled by much of today's technology. (Understanding how to reduce the time from receipt of customer order to the arrival of the system in the customers premises, from say three months to four or five days is a problem. Optimising the layout of the chips on a PCB is a puzzle. Puzzles are important but so are problems!) Is there a vision for a group workstation? Are networked systems sufficient? Probably not. Technology is needed to support team work, particularly when the teams include players who come from different worlds (e.g. marketing and manufacturing) and speak different languages (e.g. engineers and accountants).

Of course some work has been done on supporting *group work*. Computer Supported Cooperative Work (CSCW) is a relatively recent area of research activity which is concerned with supporting individuals working together using computer systems. The 'group' implied by the term cooperative work is considered to be an ensemble of people sharing a common goal and engaged in constant communication.

Much CSCW research and development effort has been directed towards office work. There is evidence however that this work has not been very successful because of its failure to take due account of the informal and social aspects of office work. Bannon and Schmidt (1989) point out that "Building computer systems where work is seen as simply being concerned with 'information flow', and neglecting the articulation work needed to make the 'flow' possible, can lead to serious problems. Computer support of cooperative work should aim at supporting self organisation of cooperative ensembles as opposed to *disrupting cooperative work by computerising formal procedures*". Later in the same article the authors criticise a CSCW project management support tool for assuming that "what people do in many situations is to follow procedures. No wonder .... the difficulty involved in developing and 'debugging' the formal protocol". Bannon and Schmidt argue that a CSCW system "supporting cooperative work involving decision making should enhance the ability of cooperating workers to interrelate their partial and parochial knowledge and facilitate the expression and communication of alternative perspectives on a given problem"; and further that the "realities of organisational life must be investigated seriously if CSCW is to be turned from a fascinating laboratory research activity into an activity producing useful systems"; finally that "the Office Automation experience has unequivocally demonstrated that the potential in terms of productivity, flexibility, product quality, etc. of information technology cannot be realised without a corresponding change in the allocation of tasks among staff."

Essentially the designers of CSCW systems *do not merely design a computer system, but in fact design work organisations*. As Bannon and Schmidt point out there is a need for a theoretical framework that help designers to understand the complex interactions between the technical subsystem, the work organisation, and the requirements of the task environment.

It is worth noting that this insight is not confined to academic researchers but is shared by at least some of commercial people. For instance a full page advertisement in the UK Sunday Times of March 27th 1988 which announced "a breakthrough in office automation management", included the following paragraph :"The effectiveness of your office depends on the *interaction of your people, their tasks, the technology they use, the way they are organised, their direction, the information they share and their surroundings. Technology is not enough.*"

2.3 COMPUTERS IN MANUFACTURING

The lessons which Bannon and Schmidt have drawn from a study of CSCW applied to the Office Automation world, can also be usefully applied in the world of manufacturing. Manufacturing systems researchers and analysts have applied computer technology widely to automate manufacturing, but the results have frequently been disappointing. This applies particularly to certain types of computer based systems in manufacturing. By and large the 'small systems', i.e. the CNC machines, the automatic assembly machines have performed as expected. However the 'larger applications', particularly those involving many people across the manufacturing plant have been less successful. A simple mechanism for categorising computer applications in manufacturing will now be examined as a way of developing this argument.

2.3.1 The Role of Computers in Manufacturing

Various schemes can be used to categorise the role of computers in manufacturing. One such scheme is to consider the nature of the computer interface to the production process. This interface may be indirect, in which case the computer's role is that of an information and decision support system, without any capability to directly sense the process. The computer system therefore manipulates information that humans have extracted from the manufacturing process and fed into the computer. Alternatively, the interface between the production process and the computer may be direct with the computer itself directly monitoring and actively controlling sections of the manufacturing process.

Examples of direct applications of the computer include CNC, Direct Numerical Control (DNC) and robotics. On the other hand, Computer Aided Process Planning, Computer assisted Numerical Control programming and computerised production management are typical examples of indirect applications.

A second scheme of classifying the role of computers in manufacturing is to distinguish between applications at the plant level and those at the operation level. Applications at plant level include computerised production management, computerised financial and accounting systems and AS/RS (Automatic Storage and Retrieval Systems). Applications at the operations level include CNC machines, computer supported work measurement systems, computer based semi-automatic and automatic assembly equipment for example, VCD (Variable Centre Distance), DIP (Dual In-line Package) and robotic equipment for inserting components into printed circuit boards in the electronics assembly industry.

Using these two axes namely, the nature of the computer interface to the process, and the level of application, a matrix of computer applications in manufacturing can be drawn up. This matrix is presented in Figure 2.3 below.

Two technologies mentioned in Figure 2.3, namely Production Management Systems and CAD systems will now be briefly examined. These two applications have been selected since they each have important consequences for the way work is carried out in the manufacturing system.

	Indirect Application	Direct Application
Plant Level	• Macro Planning Models • Accounting Systems • Production Management Systems • Computer Aided Design	• Computer Aided Warehousing • Direct Numerical Control • Flexible Manufacturing Systems • Automatic Storage and Retrieval
Operations Level	• Computer Aided Process Planning • Computer Aided Work Measurement • Computer Aided NC Programming	• Computer Aided Testing • Computer Numerical Control • Computer Based Automatic Assembly Machines • Robots

Figure 2.3: Role of Computers in Manufacturing

2.3.2 Production Management Systems

In general terms Production Management Systems are concerned with the planning and control of production in a manufacturing systems. They are frequently seen in terms of a hierarchy of subsystems; namely *strategic subsystems* which involve business planning and master scheduling systems and result in a statement of products to be manufactured by the systems over the medium term; *tactical subsystems* which are concerned with the creation of detailed plans in terms of the purchasing and production components required to meet the requirements of the master schedule; and finally *short term control subsystems* which seek to realise the plans developed by the tactical subsystem.

There are essentially two widely used approaches to production management in use in industry, namely the MRP (Materials Requirements Planning) and the JIT (Just In Time) approach. The MRP approach, which originated from IBM in the US in the mid 1960s can be considered to be a technical approach, which is based on the processing power and speed of computer technology. By now there are hundreds of MRP (or more recently MRP II, Manufacturing Resource Planning) systems available on the market and indeed thousands installed in industrial plants.

However there have been many disappointing MRP installations. Lawrence (1986) reports on a major U.K. based study of CAPM (Computer Aided Production Management) systems which showed that of 33 companies studied only 16 claimed to have successfully implemented systems - "Users do not seem to understand fully the facilities that are being offered to them in increasingly complex CAPM - Computer Aided Production Management- systems. Production controllers do not, on the whole, use the sophisticated algorithms for production scheduling made available to them in CAPM packages." Many authors have tried to understand the background to MRP success and indeed failure. It seems to be generally agreed that failure of an MRP installation can be traced to problems such as:

. Lack of top management commitment to the project;

. Lack of education in MRP for those who will have to use the system;

. Unrealistic master production schedules;

. Inaccurate data, particularly Bill of Materials data and inventory data.

Top Management Commitment

Commitment by top management is seen as *essential* to the success of any MRP installation. Undertaking the installation of an MRP system is a major decision for any manufacturing company. It has implications for many areas throughout the manufacturing organisation, for engineering in terms of the need for accurate and completely up to date Bills of Materials, for purchasing in terms of generating accurate purchase lead times, and for the materials and production people in terms of the discipline necessary to maintain accurate inventory data and working to the schedule.

Safizadeh and Raafat (1986) among other authors point to the fact that there are formal and informal systems within a manufacturing environment - "At the time of MRP implementation, a well established *somewhat accurate*, informal system is confronted with the demands and requirements of a new formal system. The installation of MRP may foster improved operations or it may lead to resistance and disintegration." As the authors point out, MRP is inevitably about trying to use accurate and timely data and rigorous procedures in the production and inventory management function. This often involves a *culture* change for a group of people, in particular shop floor supervisors, or managers, or both, and *progress chasers* who have evolved a relatively efficient and well tried manual informal system of shortage lists and priority schemes.

Latham (1981) argues that MRP "touches in some way, all the functionaries in an organisation from the chief stock clerk to the chief executive officer, and that within most manufacturing organisations, MRP threatens long established habits and prerogatives which are born out of necessity and informal systems." Latham goes on to appeal to production and inventory management professionals to learn "additional skills, skills in dealing with the human aspects of systems."

It is clear that if the manufacturing organisation is to gain all of the potential benefits of introducing MRP, management must accept the responsibility for creating the environment which is amenable to, indeed positive in its support for, the changes which MRP implementation involves. Clearly such a favourable environment cannot be created without the full and enthusiastic involvement of top management.

Perhaps successful installation is most likely to be achieved by allowing the formal MRP system and the relatively informal pre-MRP system to sit side by side over a short period. The thinking is that those who have worked the informal system have the opportunity to gradually become involved in the new MRP system, while not feeling overawed or even threatened by it. However it requires capable, sensitive and well informed management to ensure that all those involved gradually adapt the new formal MRP system and work together to achieve its full potential.

Education in MRP Thinking and Operation

A key element in any MRP installation is to ensure that all personnel in the company who are likely to come into contact with the MRP system should have some MRP education. Given the nature of MRP many people in the manufacturing plant are impacted by its introduction. Therefore a comprehensive MRP education programme has to be initiated to ensure that the system is used to its full potential. This is not to say that each employee from the Chief Executive Officer down has to be an MRP expert, rather that each needs to have sufficient understanding of MRP principles and operation to work with the system as required.

Hinds (1982) argues that "it is during .... the education process, ... that the success of MRP is often determined. .... Education is the first key to successful MRP implementation." He concludes that "the MRP process begins with, and its success is determined by, the education process, the goals of which are to support corporate objectives, acquire technical MRP knowledge, and create an atmosphere of company-wide cooperation."

The Need For Accurate Data

The MRP procedure is deceptively simple. After all what is involved but the calculation of net requirements from gross requirements taking the overall stock position into account, and then using some lot sizing technique to generate firm orders? Unfortunately life is not so simple. Earlier in this paper some prerequisites for MRP analysis were listed, such items as availability of inventory data, BOMs, master schedule data, etc.

Perhaps the greatest requirement of all for successful MRP installation and operation is discipline. The includes the discipline to maintain accurate stock records, the discipline to report accurately and in good time the completion of jobs and orders, and the discipline to report to the system, every event which MRP should be aware of. If stocks are withdrawn from stores then this fact should be notified to the system and the inventory status in the production data base updated accordingly. Many successful MRP installations have padlocks on the doors to the stockroom.

To conclude this short discussion on the failure of MRP installations it is worth referring to a Delphi study of manufacturing systems conducted in the early 1980s and reported by Benson et al. (1982). Among the questions the respondents in the study were asked to consider was the following one "When will two-thirds of the attempted first-time MRP installations be successful?". Quoting Benson et al., the answers were summarised as follows. "The majority of respondents believed that two thirds of the attempted first-time MRP installations would be successful by the early to mid 1980s. However, about 18% said that this would not occur until after 2000 or would never occur." Among the dissenting comments were, "requires a behaviour change which is never easy the first time", "too little understanding and too little user involvement will be the rule" and "people are the problem - experience and education must increase greatly before this will occur."

These comments can be summarised by saying that the failure of MRP installations is very frequently a failure to involve people in the development and installation. The emphasis on *development* is important because it is clear to many people in manufacturing that these systems must be developed around the unique requirements of individual plants and also should complement rather than seek to supplant the knowledge and intelligence of human beings.

2.3.3 The JIT Approach

An alternative approach to PMS is that of JIT (Just In Time). The success of Japanese firms in the international market place has generated an interest by many western companies in how this success was achieved. Many claim that the keystone of the Japanese success in manufacturing is Just in Time. Just in Time (JIT) is a manufacturing philosophy with a very simple goal, i.e. to produce the required items at the required quality and in the required quantities at the precise time they are needed.

The JIT system arose initially in the Toyota automotive plants in Japan in the early 1960's, and is currently being used in a variety of industries, including automotive, aerospace, machine tools, computer and telecommunications manufacturing.

The JIT Approach involves a continuous commitment to the pursuit of excellence in all phases of manufacturing systems design and operation. JIT seeks to design a manufacturing system for efficient production of 100% good units. It seeks to produce only the required items, at the required time, and in the required quantities. This is probably the simplest statement of the JIT approach to manufacturing. JIT seeks to achieve the following goals (Edwards 1983):

. Zero Defects;

. Zero Set-up Time;

. Zero Inventories;

. Zero Handling;

. Zero Breakdowns;

. Zero Lead Time;

. Lot Size of One.

There are two aspects of the set of goals listed above which are worth pointing out.

First in the minds of many manufacturing or industrial engineers trained in the *Western* approach to manufacturing systems design and operation, these goals seem very ambitious, if not unattainable.

Second the attempt to consider all of these goals simultaneously is unusual in the context of the traditional approach to manufacturing systems, which is reductionist, and involves consideration of well defined aspects of the overall manufacturing problem, in fact separate sub-problems, which are tackled and *solved* as separate problems. This approach has led to the proliferation of specialists in the various manufacturing functions, with a resulting absence of any generalist to consider the whole of the manufacturing system. The JIT approach can clearly be characterised as holistic at least in terms of the range of goals it sets for itself.

JIT seeks *Zero Defects*. The zero defects approach involves a continuous commitment to totally eliminate all waste, including in this context, yield losses and rework due to product or process defects. The methods used to achieve zero defects are those of continuous steady improvement of the production process. Schneidermann (1986) offers an interesting analysis of the process of continuous improvement towards zero defects and suggests that it should be contrasted with an alternative improvement process - the innovation process. On the one hand the continuous improvement route involves groups seeking small steps forward on a broad range of issues, using the available know-how within the group. The innovation process on the other hand seeks to achieve *great leaps forward* in narrowly defined areas through the use of science and technology by well qualified individuals. This is evidence of the JIT approach being a systems approach with clear emphasis on involvement by all of those directly concerned.

2.3.4 JIT Versus MRP

Western society has tended to adopt the world-view of scientific method, which is reductionist, quantitative and analytic in nature. The major tenet of this approach is that the whole can be reduced to its constituent parts and each examined on its own. In this manner, it is assumed that the system itself is also understood.

Such thinking is evident in the work of Adam Smith, who laid the basis for the division of labour at the beginning of the industrial revolution, and more particularly so in the case of F.W. Taylor and his approach to management at the beginning of this century. If one accepts this argument, then the approach of western manufacturing systems experts can be seen as the examination of focused well defined areas without giving due consideration to the overall system. For instance, much of the efforts of quantitative Operations Research have not had significant impact on the practice of production scheduling (see King 1976), despite the fact that there has been great energy expended over the last 20 years, since those initial influential formulations of scheduling problems, in the 1960's by researchers such as Conway et al. (1967). Moreover, writers such as Burbidge (1986) have reiterated this theme by taking issue with the over-specialised nature of manufacturing personnel.

In contrast, Eastern (i.e. Japanese) society seems more often to adopt a **systems perspective** of the world. This world-view holds that the whole is greater than the sum of its parts and so recognises the importance of interaction between the constituent sub-systems. In such a **holistic** approach, each sub-system is seen as having a certain autonomy while still operating within the overall goals of the system. The most important aspect is that no sub-system proceeds with an action which is detrimental to other sub-systems. This style of thinking is exhibited frequently in the Just in Time (JIT) approach to production management in Japan. For instance, Shingo (1981) writing on Kanban at Toyota, declares, "the following is considered quite important: (to) acknowledge the conception of **Toyota Production System**, its techniques and besides the systematic relationship between each technique."

The Western approach is perhaps best exemplified by so called **mechanistic** work organisation and work structures where individual operators tend to be assigned to a few very specialised repetitive tasks in a hierarchical supervisory environment. The alternative approach, the so called **organic** work organisation is characterised by multiskilled operators working in relatively autonomous work groups and under a less rigid control and supervisory organisation. In the author's experience the latter approach seems more appropriate, particularly in modern manufacturing systems. (The reader interested in more detailed discussion of these issues is referred to Nanda (1986), Bullinger and Ammer (1984) and Cross (1984).) A parting comment, is that since the CIM problem is primarily about integration, it follows that a holistic approach using organic work structures may well be necessary to attain a workable solution.

2.3.5 JIT - A Socio-technical Approach?

JIT appears to represent in some sense a *socio-technical* approach to production management and indeed manufacturing systems design and operation in general. For example the JIT approach to quality involves continuous improvement towards *zero defects*, with small groups actively seeking constant improvements on a broad range of issues, using the available know-how within the group. The emphasis on training and retraining of operators, on continuous improvement of the manufacturing process and on learning from past mistakes and failures to ensure that mistakes are not repeated, is further evidence of the approach.

The relative failure of many MRP installations can be explained at least partially in terms of the lack of a true socio-technical approach to the design and installation of these systems. Moreover, many of the reasons normally advanced for disappointing results from MRP appears to support the view that there is an over emphasis on the technical aspects of MRP and a failure to give due regard to the social subsystem within which the technical subsystem has to function.

The socio-technical design approach argues that the autonomy of individuals, work groups, their work roles and the social structure within which they find themselves are components of the organisation design and structure which should be addressed while the technical subsystems are under development. This approach argues that the design of the social and technical subsystems must be such as to achieve a *best fit* between the two.

The design and installation of a production management system within CIM is not a purely technical problem. Latham (1981), when he appeals to production and inventory management professionals to learn "additional skills, skills in dealing with the human aspects of systems", makes a point with which the author completely agrees. In a CIM environment, with a relatively small, highly trained workforce, the need for this socio-technical approach is even more critical.

2.3.6 CAD Systems

In the context of OKP the task of manufacturing management changes considerably. Prior to OKP, management were concerned with the development of systems to manage *routine tasks* well. With OKP the challenge is to *manage variety*. Whereas traditional technology (i.e. automation in the sense of robots, FMS etc.) removed humans from the process, new technology (the technology to support OKP) must enhance and enrich human capability.

This represents a major departure for the technology suppliers. Consider CAD systems. *Does access to a CAD system help a designer to arrive at the solution he would have arrived at without CAD only more quickly, or, does it help him or her to arrive at the optimum solution?* The author believes the former to be the case. Consider Figure 2.4 below. An engineer looking for a solution to a design problem should, in theory, search the total solution space and select the optimum solution. In practice due to constraints of time, lack of imagination, poor training etc. the engineer will likely search a restricted subset of the possible solution space and select the best solution within that limited subset. But what if the optimum solution lies outside that restricted subset?

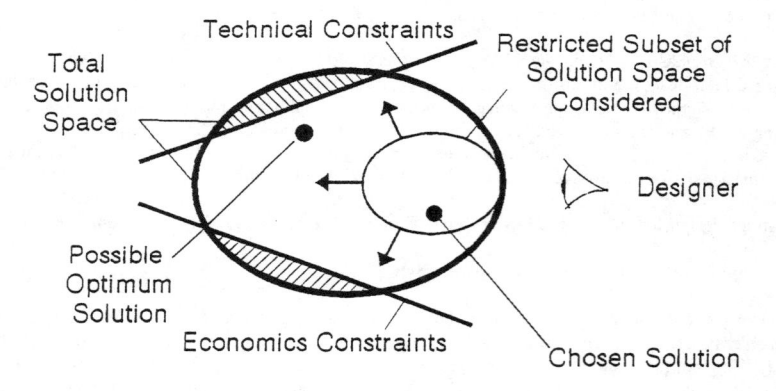

Figure 2.4: Expand the Solution Space Searched

CAD systems tend more towards helping engineers to search the restricted subset more quickly. A good CAD system should expand the range of solutions considered by the designer, rather than simply allow him to step through a restricted subset of possible solutions more quickly. In an OKP environment good CAD systems will be needed, i.e. systems which will enhance the ability to manage variety by supporting human creativity. The power of the individual must be augmented to make him more effective (doing the right things) rather than simply more efficient (doing ordinary things more quickly).

2.4 POSSIBLE RESEARCH THEMES

Today many research programmes focus on the automation of manufacturing, and try to support work in 'joining' information technology (IT) and advanced manufacturing technology (AMT). It is not sufficient however to build research projects exclusively around IT and AMT. There is a need to add a third element; namely the study of work systems, drawing in insights from disciplines such as industrial sociology, psychology including cognitive psychology and organisation design. A research programme drawing together experts from these three areas might help to prepare for the emerging OKP environment.

Moreover, looking back to Figure 2.3 presented earlier, which offered an overview of computer applications in manufacturing, it appears that it might be worth considering research themes in terms of the plant level applications and the operations level application. In this context the operations level issues are less important than the plant level issues.

Research themes will be presented under four headings, the first three of which relate to plant level issues:

. The Design Cycle;

. The Manufacturing Planning and Control Cycle;

. The Learning Organisation;

. The Manufacturing Process.

2.4.1 Research Themes on the Design Cycle

A number of ideas spring to mind. For example:

1. Is it possible to develop CAD systems which encourage human creativity rather than simply speed up the design process. The OKP environment needs creativity and fast response.

2. To date the emphasis has been on CAD-CAM integration. Can systems be developed which support customer driven design, and customer driven configuration of product to match customer expectations. This is not to support the existing *engineer to order* type environments; rather it should support an emerging OKP environment where the customer 'designs the product', for example, 'bespoke' consumer goods such as clothes, footwear, health products including for example hip replacements. Design systems can be envisaged - in the broadest sense - which support customer driven design and manufacturing.

3. What about design for the total life cycle? How should designers design for disassembly, or for scrap?

2.4.2 The Manufacturing Planning and Control Cycle

There is clear evidence, as was pointed out earlier in this chapter, that existing approaches to planning and control problems, i.e. the installation of MRP type systems, have given rise to problems in industry. People argue that JIT is inappropriate in a non Japanese environment. Can hybrid production planning and control systems be developed which draw from the MRP and JIT paradigms, and which incorporate the people centred ideas as well as the continuous improvement approach of JIT?

Within production planning and control systems, traditionally there has been a clear separation between the planners and the shop floor. With the development of focused factory and product oriented manufacturing cells, it is appropriate to pass responsibility down to the lowest level in the traditional hierarchy. Can decentralised production planning and control systems be developed which involve supervisors and operators more directly in the planning and control of the work and products they are responsible for? Can organisational structures be created which enable this to happen?

Can technology based systems be developed which support the involvement of users and the use of their local knowledge in the creation of plant schedules? What combination of scientific and operations research techniques, decision support systems, end user computing technology, and AI techniques is appropriate to realise this goal? Is it possible to move from a technology push situation to an end user (e.g. supervisor) pull situation in developing scheduling aids at all levels in the production planning and control hierarchy of systems?

2.4.3 The Learning Organisation

The OKP environment is one of constant change and fast flexible response to market requirements. To operate effectively in this environment there is a need for organisations and organisational structures which facilitate group learning and *group intelligence*. What is group intelligence? What distinguishes a successful group, or indeed company from an unsuccessful one? Can a group learn? How does a group or organisation learn, particularly when a group is composed of individuals from different disciplines, speaking different (technical) languages? How does one develop effective interdisciplinary teams who will work together to respond to customer requests and, equally important, *learn together*? How does one capture experience and make it available to new members of the group? How can the performance of a group be measured? Can individuals be motivated while at the same time encouraging group accountability? What reward systems are appropriate?

2.4.4. The Manufacturing Process

In recent years effort has been expended in developing a number of operator driven part programming systems for the part programming of CNC (computer numerically controlled) machines. Further, through the adaption of approaches such as Quality Circles, efforts have been made to involve the direct operators in the development, improvement, planning and control of the process.

The development of autonomous work groups (AWG) at the process level is encouraged by many companies today. Operators are encouraged to be more involved in the process design and development. Training approaches are required to support this development, including training of those who will be involved in the creation of the AWGs as well as the operators who will participate in them. Training traditionally has been concerned with the imparting of narrow specialised skills. Training in an OKP environment must be redefined to teach the operator to learn, to be responsive and creative.

The manufacturing process itself must be redesigned to ensure that it is ecologically acceptable. Many processes were designed within the Taylorist reductionist paradigm, e.g. the separation of machining into turning, milling, grinding etc. and the development of associated lathes, milling machines, grinders etc. Could manufacturing processes be reevaluated in the light of the move towards OKP, and the fact that our workforce today is by and large well educated and have higher expectations in terms of personal satisfaction, etc.?

2.5 CONCLUSIONS

This chapter has outlined the pressures which are being placed on the manufacturing firm in terms of dealing with product variety, short customer lead times and customers expectations with respect to price and quality. There is a trend towards OKP (One of a Kind Production) and manufacturing systems must be extremely adaptable to deal with this situation. Technology is necessary but not sufficient to achieve adaptability. The development of work systems which support human creativity, in particular work systems which enhance group creativity is essential.

Based on a very simple analysis of the experience of manufacturing systems with production management systems and with CAD systems, it is becoming clear to many researchers and practitioners that a 'technology push' solution leads to relative failure or at best a failure to realise the full potential of the system.

Kidd (1989) talks about the need for skill enhancing or skill based systems. *For business reasons* the retention and development of human skill is critical in OKP environments, and skill based systems are therefore important. Also to make better use of people there is a need to create supportive work organisations. Advanced work organisations will be based on a very flat organizational structure, decentralisation of control and decision making and a significant degree of competence at the lower levels. The author's experience in the electronics industry suggests that this is now widely recognised in industry and further that it is being implemented in for example modern product based manufacturing cells and associated Production Activity Control systems.

Brödner(1989) states that "Work design rather than pure system design has to become the main focus." The author agrees with this. The experience of Office Automation and CSCW alluded to earlier in this chapter confirms the correctness of this position.

In terms of training, Brödner (1989) observes that "traditional training concepts aim at the provision of skills and knowledge for a lifetime .... alternative concepts rather aim at providing the competence for a lifetime's learning". This can be taken a stage further. The emerging OKP environment needs **a learning organisation**. Further, there is evidence that manufacturing industry is becoming aware of this - see for example the work of Hayes, Wheelwright and Clark (1988).

CHAPTER 3

ANTHROPOCENTRIC TECHNOLOGIES: THE WAY AHEAD?

by

Professor T Husband[1]

Department of Mechanical Engineering
Imperial College of Science, Technology & Medicine
London, SW7 2BX
United Kingdom

3.1 INTRODUCTION

World class manufacturing requires, among other things, an appropriate use of advanced manufacturing technology (AMT). There is good evidence to suggest that the Japanese manufacturing industries have developed a sharp competitive edge by adopting a bottom-up approach to implementing AMT. Shop floor workers and supervisors are encouraged to influence the amount of AMT necessary to provide a balanced flow of good quality materials throughout the factory.

In Europe there is only limited adoption of bottom-up implementation of AMT although that seems to be changing rapidly. One approach which is perhaps more characteristic of a European approach concerns the use of Anthropocentric Technologies. This chapter outlines some background to the experience of Anthropocentric Technologies and proposes some future research worth pursuing to fully test these technologies and their potential for European SME's. The chapter argues that Anthropocentric Technologies could mix well with bottom-up implementation.

The first section sets out the background to anthropocentric AMT in terms of the Imperial College participation in relevant ESPRIT and UK SERC projects relating to human-centred turning cells. The second section discusses the term anthropocentric. It is concluded that it is an unhelpful term and that the best alternative is skill-based technology although that is also flawed.

In the third section some commercial justifications for investing in skill-based technology are offered. In the fourth section a number of research themes which would offer valuable underpinning for the development of skill-based technologies over the next 10-15 years are suggested. The themes are offered under three categories: technology, organisation, and people.

3.2 BACKGROUND

In recent years the implementation of Information Technology in manufacturing, in the form of advanced manufacturing technology (AMT), has been widely portrayed as the means by which to automate batch production, an area where hitherto extensive automation has not been regarded as an economic proposition. As such, AMT has been heralded as a means by which to derive the low unit cost benefits of mass production in a batch manufacturing environment. There has been an avalanche of information about various facets of AMT, including computer-aided design (CAD), computer-aided manufacture (CAM) and flexible manufacturing systems (FMS). Latterly, AMT has been largely superseded as a buzzword by

---

[1]The assistance of colleagues at Imperial College is gratefully acknowledged. This chapter draws heavily on material produced originally by Mr R-R Slatter and Ms T Hancke.

computer-integrated manufacturing (CIM) which, broadly speaking, describes the plant-wide integration of a variety of computer-aided functions and processes, such as CAD, CAM and FMS.

Whilst great benefits have been claimed for different forms of AMT, including reduced lead times, reduced work-in-progress and increased stock turnover, surveys giving the actual figures for the diffusion of AMT indicate evolutionary rather than revolutionary growth. For example, in the UK, just seven percent of the overall machine-tool population is computer-controlled (Metalworking Production 1988), and just one factory in 40 possesses a robot (Northcott et al. 1986), whilst worldwide there is estimated to be just 150-200 FMSs (Bessant and Haywood 1985) and CIM remains primarily speculative (Leonard 1988). Nevertheless, rapid growth is expected and it is not unusual to see forecasts of exponential growth for the different forms of AMT.

Various supply-side and user-side constraints on diffusion have been identified, not least the considerable costs of most forms of AMT and the particular difficulty of integrating hardware, software and organisational systems. In the particular case of FMS, though, the key factor restricting widespread adoption has been the limited applicability of the current generation of systems. Surveys indicate that not only do most FMSs lack significant product flexibility, but their high cost has primarily limited their application to large companies engaged in medium to high volume production (Bessant and Haywood 1985), this in turn guiding the development of the technology towards the needs of such companies. Accordingly, the majority of potential users, that is, small to medium sized companies engaged in small batch production, have been largely untouched by the technology. Furthermore, only a small proportion of present systems deal with rotational parts, despite the fact that in general engineering some 70 percent of components have at least one turning operation.

Moreover, it would appear that the benefits claimed could present a biased picture, because failures are seldom admitted and hardly ever publicly reported. A survey by Ingersoll Engineers of 48 FMSs found that an uncomfortably high number had failed to realise the expectations of their purchasers (Holz 1984), an experience that other studies indicate is representative for other major forms of AMT, such as CADCAM (Marsden 1986).

Much of this is the result of new technologies being implemented without careful integration into the company's business plan, that is, there is a lack of strategic planning with respect to AMT. Clegg (1988) describes the introduction of AMT in sophisticated high-tech companies as unduly technology-driven, whilst the development of AMT in less sophisticated companies is characterised by a process of muddling through. Moreover, human operators are typically viewed as sources of unpredictability and error, such that wherever possible system functions are allocated to machines rather than humans. Clegg goes on to point out that whether technology driven or designed by muddling through, little attention is paid to the human and organisational aspects of AMT until the technology has been designed and often not until it is implemented.

It should therefore be no surprise that there is increasing evidence that unforseen human and managerial problems with AMT often prove more difficult to deal with than technical problems, which although complex, are more often expected (Meredith 1987). Blumberg and Gerwin (1984) regard the lack of attention to the human and organisational aspects of AMT as responsible for a lack of fit between the demands made by the technology and the needs, skills and procedures of the human support system on which it still, ultimately, depends.

There is growing recognition of the need for **both** technology and organisational structure to be constituted so as to facilitate the coordinated and controlled pursuit of strategic objectives (Child 1987). Indeed, Stark (1988) suggests that organisational integration, by reducing organizational complexity and, thereby, substantial non value-added costs, is a pre-requisite if the full benefits of integrated technologies such as CADCAM or FMS are to be realised.

In the absence of an accepted theory on the design of organisation for AMT there is a surprising consensus in the literature as to the desirable features of the new flexible organisation, as compared to the traditional organisation associated with pre-AMT technologies, as summarised in Figure 3.1.

Flexible Organization for Flexible Technology ?	
"Traditional" Organization	**"Flexible" Organization**
● High division of labour	● Organizational Integration
● Low work value / motivation	● High work value / motivation
● Low priority for training	● Training and organizational development given high priority
● Centralized planning and decision making	● Decentralized planning and decision making
● Technology taken as "given"	● Technology shaped to meet organizational needs

Figure 3.1: Flexible Organisation for Flexible Technology?

3.2.1 Human Aspects of AMT

As indicated above, there is significant evidence that most companies adopt a technology-centred approach to system design and implementation, whereby human and organisational aspects of the technology are taken for granted. As pointed out by Clegg (1988), this can lead to sub-optimal performance for a number of reasons poor system design (that does not meet user requirements); lack of clarity, understanding and consensus about how the system will be operated and managed; poor interfaces; poor job designs and organisational structures; and inadequate training.

In the case of FMS, the shop floor end of CIM where, arguably, technological integration has progressed furthest, the typical practical situation is described by Jones (1986). His survey of FMSs in the USA and UK indicates that in most of the systems studied, inflexible and polarized pre-FMS organisational structures had been applied to the system, whereby the machine operators lost control of what was being done at their machine, the bulk of preparatory work being taken on by other personnel, such as programmers and setters. Blumberg and Gerwin (1984) describe a similar situation, in which work in the FMSs studied did not provide enough autonomy, task identity, responsibility or feedback, leading to the conclusion that work in an FMS has little potential for motivating people, is not very satisfying and is stressful.

Thus a curious paradox arises in many highly automated machine shops. Tasks are typically limited to menial machine minding activities, yet the operators are still expected to intervene, and if possible correct, in the event of a malfunction, this task requiring a high level of information processing and decision making in an FMS. This latter point is substantiated by the tendency of firms to prefer highly skilled personnel to man such systems, but, as pointed out by Corbett (1985), any system that does not provide the experience out of which operating skills can develop will be vulnerable in those circumstances where human intervention becomes necessary. Given the need for continual remedial activity in existing systems (Jones 1986), and the major effect that humans can have on system performance, by the manner in which they respond to operating and maintenance faults, it would seem imperative that the motivation and satisfaction of operating and maintenance personnel be considered carefully.

Further research into the human aspects of AMT raises a number of other points also relevant to the author's research. First, the operation of AMT, in the form of, say, CNC machine tools, is less distinctive for requiring specific information technology skills, than advanced machining skills. This reflects the fact that computer control, in the form of CNC, enables the control of a more demanding machining process, so requiring an evolution of traditional skills, and that it is the machining process itself that brings forth the bulk of working problems and attractions alike (Sorg et al. 1983).

Secondly, there is considerable choice in the organisation of work around AMT. For example, stand-alone CNC machine tools are compliant in the sense that they can be programmed either at the machine or from an office and, moreover, can allow modifications of work organisation to take place after the machines have been installed. However, for more integrated systems, such as FMS, the situation is quite different. Here the impact that the system will have on managers and workers at all levels of the organisation becomes more predetermined and the shape of the organisation and individual skills and responsibilities may be constrained by the design of the system. This can mean that it becomes harder for organisations to adapt to changing circumstances and evolve over time (Burnes and Fitter 1987).

Thus information technology in manufacturing must be regarded as both a constraint and opportunity for promoting organisational change. The potential of AMT as a **vehicle** for organisational change has been recognised by some companies, who have used FMS as a catalyst to instigate organisational changes to achieve 'Japanese-style' labour flexibility with multi-skilled shop floor workers responsible for their own quality control (Bessant and Haywood 1985). But the vast majority of companies are not so enlightened, choosing instead default options, such that jobs and local organisational structures are designed as they were with old technologies, with minimum levels of skill and responsibility and with highly differentiated structures respectively.

The technology-centred approach to system design has a further, critical, dysfunctional effect. Not only does system productivity depend directly on the skill of the operators, but the human element in AMT is also responsible for vital flexibility. Current market characteristics of increasing part variety, demands for shorter delivery times and decreasing product life cycles, place great premium on the added flexibility offered by human involvement in the manufacturing process. There is thus the possibility of a further paradox, whereby a company can own exemplary automated factories and still lose its competitiveness, because the high capital investments already undertaken are in fact restricting the strategic flexibility of the company (Warnecke 1988).

3.2.2 Research into the Design of AMT with a Human Orientation

Many of the human problems of work design associated with FMS are similar to those identified in the past in highly structured environments, such as mass production flow-lines. In both cases jobs often involve low levels of control over work methods and pace, and high levels of attention and cognitive demand, resulting in turn in high levels of stress and low levels of job satisfaction and motivation. There is a substantial knowledge-base documenting the past efforts of psychologists, ergonomists and sociologists to humanise work, but much of this research suffers from fundamental limitations when considered with regard to the design and implementation of AMT. First, as implied above, most of the work has been concentrated on mass production environments, with little attention to batch production. Secondly, and more importantly, the bulk of previous work in this area has been retrospective and therefore has not dealt with the design of the technology, which has been taken as given.

As has been pointed out above, this determinist line of thought does not apply to AMT, where there is a degree of choice as to how work is organised around the technology and how functions are allocated between machines and humans, though as it has also been pointed out, system design can also constrain work organisation and job design options.

It is therefore apparent that there is a need for a parallel design approach, whereby the technology is shaped by human factors considerations, aimed at ensuring the psychological well-being of the system operators as well as organisational effectiveness, by facilitating the development of a flexible organisation as outlined in Figure 3.1.

Various alternative parallel approaches to the design and implementation of new technologies have been proposed, but the most widely known is the so called human-centred approach pioneered by Rosenbrock (1984). There is no concise definition of human-centred AMT, since the approach is more a philosophy than a set of rigid rules, but a number of key features can be listed:

. the technology should take account of the existing skills of the user and should provide the user with the opportunity to learn, so as to further develop these skills;

. the technology should facilitate the maximisation of operator choice and control;

. human-centred AMT should integrate the planning, execution and monitoring components of work, so minimising the subdivision of work;

. the technology should be designed such that operator knowledge of the whole production process is maximised;

. the technology should encourage social communication and interaction between its users;

. the technology should readily form part of a healthy, safe and efficient working environment.

Over and above the benefits of organisational integration and the avoidance of the problems of the technology-led approach, the adoption of a human-oriented approach is expected to give a variety of further benefits. First, the design of the system may be better if users can be involved in the design process, since the system is more likely to suit their particular needs, or because they have important job-specific knowledge which should be included. Second, if man-machine interfaces are poorly designed, operator training inadequate, or support from programmers and planners inadequate, then the system is unlikely to fulfil its potential. A human-oriented approach offers the possibility of avoiding problems and, if the human aspects are well managed, the system is likely to reach performance targets more quickly than would otherwise be the case (Clegg and Corbett 1987).

3.2.3 Relevant Research at Imperial College

Initial research at the University of Manchester Institute of Science and Technology (UMIST), under the supervision of Professor Rosenbrock, resulted in the development of software for a human-centred control system for a CNC lathe, and this research has been continued as part of ESPRIT project 1199 entitled 'Human-Centred CIM Systems'. This project, which commenced in May 1986, involved partners in three countries. A German group developed a factory information system for production planning and control, whilst the Danish group developed a human-centred CAD system. The British group developed prototype turning cells incorporating human-centred CNC lathes and automated workhandling equipment, to be installed at user sites for industrial trials.

In December 1986 a complementary project began at Imperial College, entitled 'The Operation and Management of Flexible Human-Centred Turning Cells'. This project is funded by the Science and Engineering Research Council in addition to four industrial partners, including companies from the machine tool, computer and control system industries. The centrepiece of the project, as suggested by its title, is a flexible human-centred turning cell, consisting of a CNC lathe, CNC milling machine, with associated workhandling and inspection equipment. This demonstrator cell fulfils a dual role as a vehicle for testing hardware and software developed according to human-centred guidelines, as well as a test bed for assessing the suitability of a human-centred cell for one of the project's industrial partners. As will be seen later the cell, which is capable of completely machining a wide range of rotational components, forms the shop-floor end of a human-centred CIM system currently being developed at Imperial College.

Figure 3.2 shows how human factors considerations provide a framework of design guidelines for the design of man-machine systems, such as the demonstrator turning cell. Where possible existing social science guidelines, from areas such as socio-technical system design, ergonomics and participative systems design, have been used, though in some cases reformulated to make them more accessible to production and system engineers, who will ultimately have the greatest influence on system design and implementation.

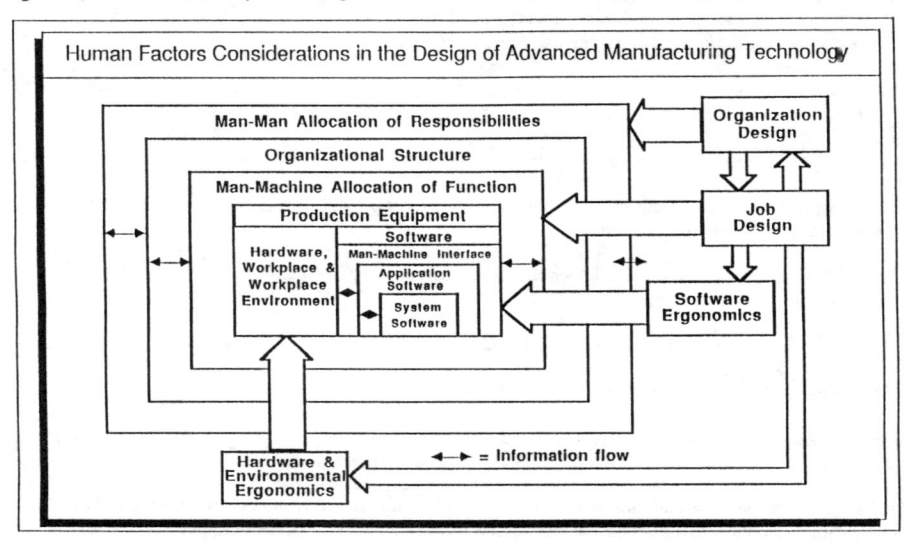

Figure 3.2: Human Factors Considerations in the Design of Advanced Manufacturing Technology

Figure 3.3 shows the parallel design procedure adopted during the design of the various hardware and software elements constituting the demonstrator human-centred CIM facility, which includes human-centred production planning and control and human-centred CADCAM software, as described in more detail in Besant et al. (1988).

Some of the main research issues in this project are:

. the development of a sample solution for a particular user site;

. the testing and evaluation of this solution;

. the evaluation of costs and benefits of the adopted solution;

. an assessment of the transferability of the solution and the validity of the human-centred concept as adopted here;

. an assessment of the training requirements;

. the demonstration (if possible) of the economic competitiveness of the concept and its superiority in other aspects (such as job satisfaction).

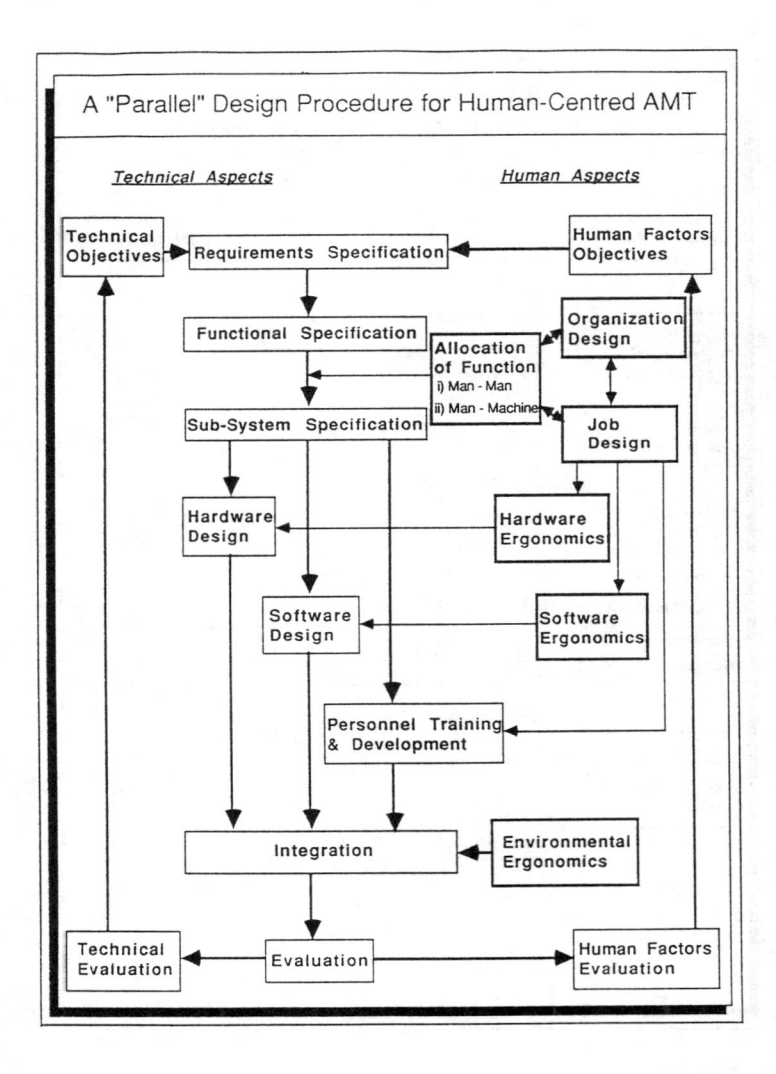

Figure 3.3: A Parallel Design Procedure for Human Centred AMT

Human-Centred Cell Software

The cell has been designed prospectively for use by multi-skilled flexible craftsmen, who manage all activities within the cell; they are not merely trouble shooters or machine loaders required to make the system work. Figure 3.4 shows the different tasks to be undertaken by the cell operators, who will work in a semi-autonomous work group, a work design indicated to be particularly appropriate for this implementation of AMT by the socio-technical framework proposed by Cummings and Blumberg (1987).

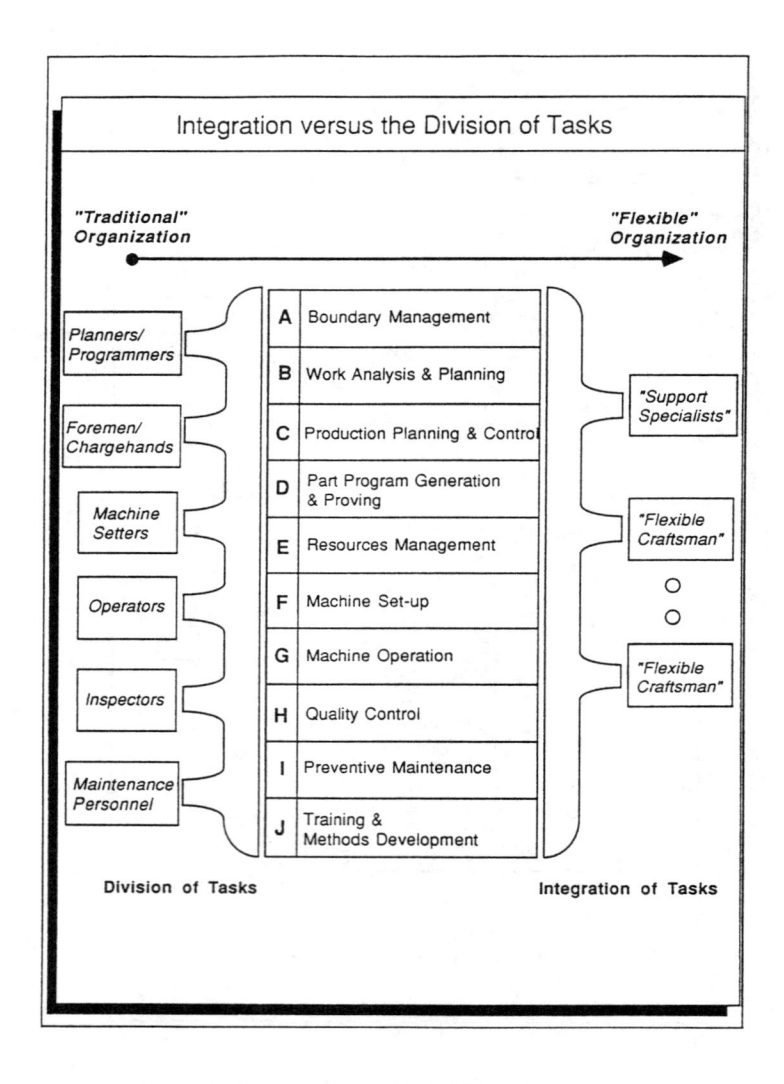

```
┌─────────────────────────────────────────────────────────┐
│           Integration versus the Division of Tasks       │
│                                                          │
│   "Traditional"                              "Flexible"  │
│   Organization                              Organization │
│   ●────────────────────────────────────────────────▶    │
│                                                          │
│                    ┌───┬──────────────────────┐          │
│                    │ A │ Boundary Management  │          │
│   ┌──────────────┐ ├───┼──────────────────────┤ ┌──────┐ │
│   │ Planners/    │ │ B │ Work Analysis &      │ │"Support│
│   │ Programmers  │ │   │ Planning             │ │Special-│
│   └──────────────┘ ├───┼──────────────────────┤ │ists"  │
│   ┌──────────────┐ │ C │ Production Planning  │ └──────┘ │
│   │ Foremen/     │ │   │ & Control            │          │
│   │ Chargehands  │ ├───┼──────────────────────┤          │
│   └──────────────┘ │ D │ Part Program         │          │
│   ┌──────────────┐ │   │ Generation & Proving │ ┌──────┐ │
│   │ Machine      │ ├───┼──────────────────────┤ │"Flex-│ │
│   │ Setters      │ │ E │ Resources Management │ │ible  │ │
│   └──────────────┘ ├───┼──────────────────────┤ │Crafts│ │
│   ┌──────────────┐ │ F │ Machine Set-up       │ │man"  │ │
│   │ Operators    │ │   │                      │ └──────┘ │
│   └──────────────┘ ├───┼──────────────────────┤    ○     │
│                    │ G │ Machine Operation    │    ○     │
│   ┌──────────────┐ │   │                      │ ┌──────┐ │
│   │ Inspectors   │ ├───┼──────────────────────┤ │"Flex-│ │
│   └──────────────┘ │ H │ Quality Control      │ │ible  │ │
│                    ├───┼──────────────────────┤ │Crafts│ │
│                    │ I │ Preventive           │ │man"  │ │
│   ┌──────────────┐ │   │ Maintenance          │ └──────┘ │
│   │ Maintenance  │ ├───┼──────────────────────┤          │
│   │ Personnel    │ │ J │ Training & Methods   │          │
│   └──────────────┘ │   │ Development          │          │
│                    └───┴──────────────────────┘          │
│                                                          │
│       Division of Tasks            Integration of Tasks  │
└─────────────────────────────────────────────────────────┘
```

Figure 3.4: Integration Versus the Division of Tasks

Analysis of the various tasks to be carried out by the cell operators and the flow of information and material to and from the cell, resulted in a basic functional requirement for the software of the turning cell computer, based on the assumption that part programs were to be generated by the cell operators whether using human-centred CNC controllers or CAM software on the cell computer. The various functions in which the computer assists the cell operators in their management of the cell can be listed as follows:

. Cell Production Planning and Control;

. Process Planning;

. Part Program Management;

. Resources Management;

. Quality Control;

. Diagnostic Information;

. Operator Utilities.

The software structure and associated hardware for the cell computer, at the current stage of development, is shown in Figure 3.5.

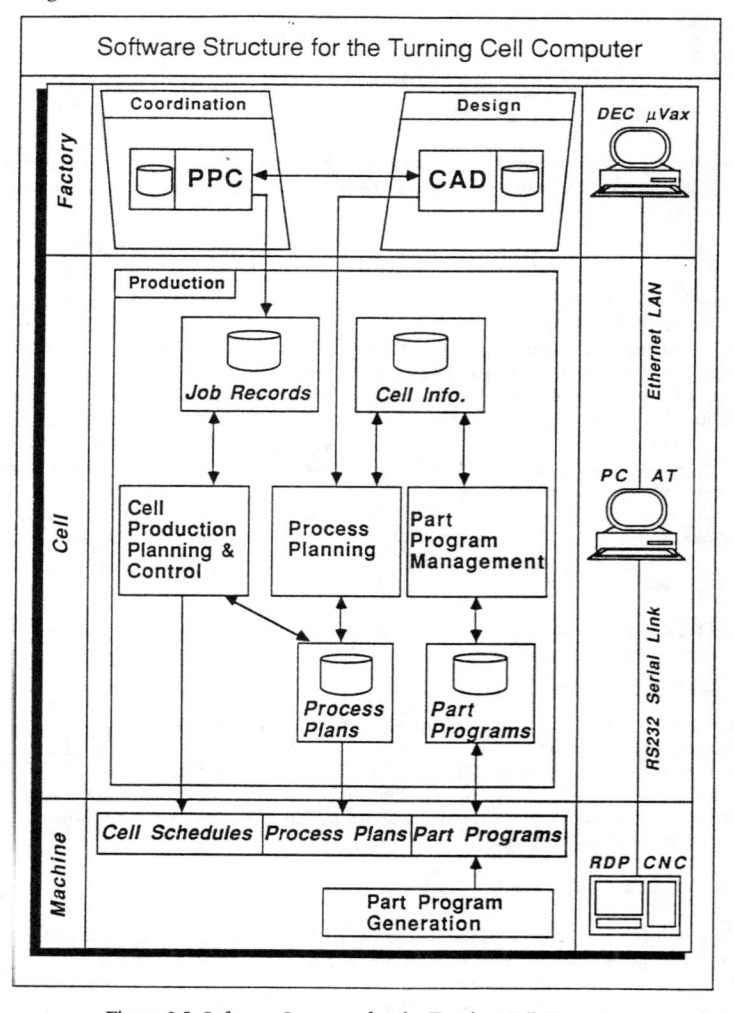

Figure 3.5: Software Structure for the Turning Cell Computer

As indicated by the diagram, a PC AT type computer provides the hardware, the particular hardware and software combination used supporting a WIMP (Windows, Icons, Mouse, Pull-down menus) colour graphics environment, which is important for man-machine interface design. Importantly, such an environment facilitates the use of direct manipulation techniques, which are an effort to present and manipulate information in a manner that matches the way in which the user thinks. This choice of hardware also supports serial communications to and from the CNC control units of the cell's machines, as well as providing the capability for communicating with computers on different levels in the overall system hierarchy, as shown in Figure 3.5.

It can be seen that the development of the cell computer software to date has concentrated on three applications:

. Process Planning;

. Part Program Management;

. Cell Production Planning and Control.

In developing these packages particular attention has been paid to making the operation of the software transparent to the operator and also to making the software suitable for use by personnel of differing skill levels.

Process Planning

In the demonstrator CIM facility, the factory level production planning and control system (PPC) is responsible for the routing of jobs to particular cells, whilst design geometry is passed to the cell from the factory level computer-aided design (CAD) system. This information provides the basic data for the process planning procedure, which consists of specifying the workhandling, workholding and tooling information for each component to be machined in the cell. The interactive process planning software on the cell computer enables this function to be devolved to the cell operators. The operators can define the sequence of operations, choosing from a range of workhandling, workholding and tooling options, determined by production engineering support specialists together with the cell personnel. This application package has a facility for variant process planning, whereby the user can graphically edit an existing plan for a component with similar machining requirements. Importantly, the information entered during the process planning procedure is used subsequently in production planning, for calculating machine set-up times etc.

Part Program Management

As stated earlier, the cell operators generate part programs at the machines, currently using existing CNC control systems, but ultimately using human-centred CNC control systems, or human-centred CAM software on the cell computer.

The latter is used for mass storage of part programs, which can then be stored together with important information, such as who created the program and when, whether it has been proven out, etc. Serial communication links (RS232C) provide the means of transferring programs between the cell's machine tools and the cell computer. The software incorporates direct manipulation techniques, such that the user, for example, merely needs to click on icons representing the desired part program and corresponding machine tool to transfer a program to a machine.

Cell Production Planning and Control

One of the basic principles of human-centred AMT is that the planning, execution and monitoring elements of work should be united and the cell operators are, accordingly, provided with software to help them sequence the work allocated to the cell in an interactive fashion. The cell receives a work-list as agreed with the factory level production planning function, consisting of a list of batches to be completed by a given due date. The cell operators are then free to sequence the batches in such a way as to achieve a set objective function, such as minimising set-up times, to minimise the makespan for a particular list of jobs. To facilitate this task, the software offers a variety of heuristic scheduling rules, such that the user can re-order the batches as he chooses and can run the display section of the package as a simulator to answer what-if? enquiries. This facility can also be used as a capacity planning tool when accepting jobs from factory level production planning. The cell schedule is displayed as a Gantt chart, which can be further manipulated by the operator to fine tune the schedule.

Importantly, the software is also used for production control purposes, in that the operator notifies the cell computer when a particular job is started or completed and can also enter the actual times taken to, say, machine a particular component, or prepare the corresponding part programs. Not only does this mean that the planned cell schedule is constantly being brought into line with the actual state of production, but this information will also be stored in the computer's job records database, which can be read by factory level production planning to provide feedback on cell performance.

3.2.4 ESPRIT Project 1199: Human-Centred CIM

This project finished in September 1989. However, as it is widely perceived to be a key project in the field of human-centred design it will briefly be described here.

The main objectives of the project were to:

. establish criteria for the design of human-centred CIM systems;

. develop a manufacturing system that achieves a high level of flexibility and robustness in CIM systems and provides a better work environment;

. define the training for a new type of multi-skilled worker;

. demonstrate the economic and commercial competitiveness of the human-centred CIM concept.

The partners in the project were from Denmark, Germany and the UK and included universities and industrial companies. Two demonstrator production cells were to be developed:

1. a CNC turning cell with two lathes at Rolls-Royce (from which the concept for the Imperial College cell was derived);

2. a product-oriented production island at BICC Sealectro (now ITT Sealectro).

BICC's production island was developed for the production of radio frequency connectors. The demonstrator cell comprised a mixed set of machines and equipment among them a CNC-lathe and a second operation machine. The operations performed in the island included turning, milling, boring, curing, heat treatment, inspection, and assembly.

The work in the project covered amongst other items:

. specification of business requirements;

. design of the production island layout;

. computer hardware and software architecture;

. evaluation and modification of suggested job descriptions;

. training issues;

. user involvement;

. implementation of a human-centred system;

. system demonstration;

. preliminary cost benefit evaluation (at the end of project).

Some of the findings from this project (most of which are true for the SERC project) are:

. the interdisciplinary cooperation between social scientists and engineers might be difficult at times, but it is always refreshing, innovative and thus important, and it has to be continued (see also Kidd and Corbett 1988);

. as in the SERC project, the need to specify the technical hardware in the project proposal already limited the project by actually giving it a technology-centred start;

. users should be involved from an early stage and their views and comments should influence the design;

. the concept of human-centred CIM has to be introduced very diplomatically, since giving control to the operators on the shop floor and having them participate in the development and implementation of a new system might seem unfavourable or even dangerous to the management involved;

. a general change in attitude has to take place with all people involved, not only management, to acknowledge the benefits of this approach, for example, operator motivation and job satisfaction are not measurable, but are likely to have a stronger effect on productivity than machine utilisation figures.

3.3 TERMINOLOGY: IS ANTHROPOCENTRIC A HELPFUL LABEL?

The terminology used to describe the underlying philosophy of industrial strategy is important. It could be argued that Just-in-Time (JIT), the phrase coined by the Japanese is a good example of successful labelling. The term captures the essence of the underlying philosophy and is simple to understand. Over the years there have been attempts to devise similar, simple terms to describe other relatively complex issues. Some have been disastrous, others helpful if not spectacularly so.

Take the example of Tribology. When academics and industrialists struggled in the 1960's to find a single term to sum up this wide-ranging area of engineering, they approached the Greek scholars who suggested the word tribos or wear. Hence tribology. For many workers in the field the term has proved helpful in that it gets across, in a single word, the technologies relating to a multi-disciplinary field of huge strategic importance to the engineering industry as a whole.

In the 1970's when the British government decided to raise the awareness of industry to the need for improved plant maintenance strategies they also looked to the Greek scholars. It was explained that maintenance meant the total process of designing, buying, operating and owning a physical resource e.g. machine tool, building or delivery truck. The scholars suggested the Greek word terin (to protect or to guard) as a basis. Hence the term Terotechnology was conceived and promoted widely by the British Government's Department of Trade & Industry and by consultants, academics and engineers in many other countries. It proved to be a failure. The term was too clumsy, difficult to explain and fell into fairly early disuse.

How about Anthropocentric? It is likely to fall into the same category as Terotechnology - clumsy, difficult to explain and not helpful. It is likely to disappear quickly.

It **would** be useful to devise a term analogous to JIT to convey the basis of human-oriented systems of manufacture. An obvious danger is that the terminology will be so simplistic as to mislead. Take for example the term user-friendly which is quite clearly not a correct description but is, sadly, used by some commentators.

People-based technology is a possible term but it does not get to the heart of the matter. Clegg (1988) uses appropriate technology which is better but does not summon up the real dimensions of the problem. Appropriate is also used to describe other technologies, eg that suitable for Third World Countries.

Human-centred, the term used at Imperial College, is acceptable but, like people-based lacks incisiveness. The concept to be emphasised is the need for human skills to be incorporated into advanced manufacturing systems.

As a result, and after much thought, the author would go along with Kidd's (1989) proposal that skill-based system is the best available at present. Nevertheless the term has a major flaw. The implication of skill-based could be that skills are being emphasised to the detriment of technology when, of course, we are seeking to describe systems which balance technocentric and socio-centric. The unhappy conclusion is that the search for a really helpful label might be futile.

3.4 COMMERCIAL AND TECHNICAL JUSTIFICATIONS

It would be sad, and quite wrong, if skill-based technology was to be seen as a matter only for academics - and social scientists in particular. It is not. There are crucially important reasons why European industry should understand and implement this technology so as to retain and improve its profitability and its market share.

There are some promising achievements already. Consider ESPRIT project 1199.

3.4.1 BICC Sealectro

Hamlin (1989b) has produced a preliminary cost-benefit analysis of the work described briefly in Section 3.2.

The business objectives set out at the beginning of the project were:

1. improvement of customer due date performance;

2. reduction of manufacturing lead time;

3. reduction of working capital, and

4. reduction of operating expenses.

A computer-based simulation of a human-centred CIM production island at Sealectro has been performed and compared with actual performance data over a period of 13 weeks. For comparison, the personnel and machine resources were the same for both islands. Further assumptions covered the same order volume, a continuous raw material flow, and production in relatively small batches. Effects of machine breakdowns etc. could not be assessed in detail, however, in the worst case of excess working hours, the results for the simulation still represented an improvement over the actual performance.

For the adopted configuration of the island based on Optimised Production Technology, Period Batch Control, and Human-Centred CIM, the following results were obtained.

1. Due date performance: Due date performance increased by 55 percent (based on number of orders).

	Early	On Time	Late
Existing Island	18%	31%	51%
Simulation	14%	86%	0%

2. Reduction of lead time:

The reduction of lead time is indicated by the reduction of the average work in-progress levels, expressed in Weeks of Sales (WOS):

existing island: 2.45 WOS
simulation: 1.12 WOS

Lead time was halved, while throughput doubled.

3. Reduction of working capital:

The relative value of the overall average work in-progress was reduced by 45 percent.

4. Reduction of operating expenses:

Excess working hours were reduced by 75 percent. Further reductions in costs can be expected in connection with this.

These benefits reflect only the different form of organisation (such as de-centralisation, operator control (here planning)) and the direct effects of the CIM implementation. The full benefits from the integration of the knowledge and experience of the operator are not included here, as the computer simulation does not readily accommodate these. The actual overall performance of such a system can only be derived from actual operating results. It will be interesting to see eventually how the actual results of such an island will compare with the conventional island and the forecasted simulation results. However, it will be another six months or a year yet before further results will be available.

3.4.2 Systems Reliability

A major cause of disappointment with advanced systems of manufacture relates to the inherent reliability of both hardware and software. Many individual system components have impressive MTBF (mean time between failure) values e.g. robots, conveyors, gantry cranes etc. But given the scale and complexity of FMS and similar systems it is not surprising that downtime is high because of the interdependence of the components.

Often the failure, however trivial and short-lived, of a single building block can lead to total shutdown of the system.

With a skilled worker (coordinator or manager) designed into the system, the scope for salvaging these problems is greatly improved. A skilled worker can diagnose by noise, smell or sight or even touch the likely failure of the majority of tools or machines. He can do so much better than any array of existing computer-based condition monitoring devices. He can also continue to operate some elements of the system even when some part of it has failed.

For the SME in any case it would be many years into the future before it could justify implementing totally unmanned systems, even if unmanned systems were feasible. Why? Simply because SME's do not have the in-house skills required to update software or to offer the range of maintenance skills necessary. SME's will continue to operate semi-automatic systems. FMS can offer great benefits, mainly in product versatility and speed of response, and with skill-based technology the SME has a realistic chance of deriving these benefits.

3.4.3 Faster Response and Greater Flexibility

To compete with world-leading manufacturers it is becoming increasingly important to reduce lead-times and to respond quickly to changing market demands.

The lessons from Japan are many. One key strategy has been to implement AMT on a bottom-up rather than top-down basis. In other words the use of shop floor and supervisory workers to identify where the automated technology is really required, to balance the flow of production, has proved a huge success. It incorporates concepts such as quality circles but involves less spectacular concepts such as effective training and worker identification with the company. In Europe there is still the tendency to impose AMT implementation from the top-down.

With skill-based technology, companies are in a stronger position to modify the products of an FMS or similar system. The skilled worker can respond to minor design changes far quicker than software-based procedures. This does not mean that advanced technology is irrelevant. It does mean that maximum benefit can be derived from it as a result of human intervention. As noted earlier, this is of particular significance to the European SME.

Reduction of lead time, improved system reliability, greater flexibility and faster response to the market are real commercial issues. Success in these directions leads to improved bottom-line performance. European industry in the next 10-15 years will increasingly face the challenges of low volume and high variety manufacture. It will also face up to decreasing product life cycles and world markets which will be more sophisticated than today.

The costs of moving to skill-based technology are not insignificant. Large investments in education and training will be necessary. Continuing ingenuity in devising artificial intelligence techniques which can be incorporated into balanced human and automation based factories will require R&D investment.

Given the future facing Europe, however, our industries cannot afford not to pursue skill based technology.

3.5 RESEARCH THEMES FOR THE FUTURE

Skill-based Technology will not be adopted effectively in Europe without strategic R&D efforts. In this section a range of relevant themes relating to Technology, Organisation and People are offered.

3.5.1 Technology

It is important to realise that skill-based systems are not anti-technology. The aim is to find the optimal blend of automation and human input. Indeed the use of advanced technology is an essential ingredient. Some technology topics which would enhance the scope of skill-based systems include:

Condition Monitoring

The use of robust diagnostic and monitoring technology in CIM is still relatively limited in comparison with, say, the process industries. There are good reasons for this. It is difficult to employ many of the well established technologies of condition monitoring in robots, conveyors or even machine tools. Research is needed to extend the use of tool wear monitoring and tool breakage diagnostics as well as to assess fail-safe software. With monitoring equipment distributed around a skill-based system the operator could exert a finer control over large-scale integrated plant. Research into the distributed computing aspects could be of particular relevance.

Free-ranging Robotic Vehicles

The use of automated guided vehicles (AGV) will increase within CIM. For a skill-based system the operator will need to work alongside and manage a small fleet of AGV's. Much more work is required to develop truly free-ranging vehicles with guaranteed safety features. Research in vehicle navigation technology and docking sensors would be highly relevant. Voice control of an AGV would also be a valuable feature.

Component Identification

The use of bar code readers is now well established but more sophisticated methodologies will be necessary for versatile, skill-based CIM. Possibly advanced vision technology (using parallel processing-based computing) could be developed to recognise every component produced in a skill-based cell.

Genetic Algorithms Applications

Genetic Algorithms (GA) are probabilistic heuristic adaptive algorithms which search for an optimum set of coadapted parameter values that represent the global optimum of a pre-defined performance space. The algorithms are called genetic because they incorporate simplified operators adapted from population genetics and natural selection in contrast to traditional analytic and numeric optimising algorithms.

Work on autonomous robot programming investigating a new approach to Machine Learning and to robot programming, could prove valuable.

The development of GA to the stage where a system might incorporate robotic-devices which can learn and improve their performance from the operator's initial teaching in an essentially autonomous fashion, would offer a further dimension to the skill-based operator's scope.

Intelligent Methodology and Simulation

The development of simulation and optimisation methods in CIM systems should gradually and eventually lead to expert selection for control of manufacture and minimise the effects of various transients, e.g. machine breakdown on this control.

Expert systems generally, for, say cutting tool selection, press tool operation sequencing, machine speeds etc. hold out significant promise. The idea would be to develop such systems for skill-based technology such that the operator can use them and, with experience, further extend them for his particular application.

Database Methodologies and Networking

Factories consisting of islands of skill-based systems will require soundly constructed databases which are easily accessed. The databases will need to be designed using intelligent structures ie in formats compatible with the way humans (and not computers) think. Development of mechanisms for on-line conversations between various areas of the factory would also be of importance.

The networking of distributed data will lie at the heart of future skill-based factories. In particular, the flow of data (real time and interactive) from factory level to cell or island level and across, to workstation level is of central importance. Extension of the Imperial College work (section 3.2) in this direction would be valuable.

Structuring Technological Choices

Development of the ideas put forward by various authors (e.g. Chalmet 1987) on the strategic choice of manufacturing technology (e.g. cell or stand-alone or fully integrated system of machines) would be worthwhile. The use of simulation procedures, incorporating human interventions, could well be a central feature of any such research.

3.5.2 Organisation

It is tempting to propose a range of R&D activities which will help to prescribe the design of optimum CIM systems. However, the point made by Corbett (1988) is valid:

"with the best will in the world, engineers cannot be expected to develop new design methods armed solely with lists of criteria, however comprehensive."

There is scope nevertheless for research into design tools to help engineers establish a good practice skill-based system methodology. Some key issues include:

Control of Skill-Based Systems

Using a framework of the kind proposed by Clegg and Corbett (1987) there is scope for research into assessing the choices available at the system design stage. For example, allocation of function or responsibilities (use functional specialist or the operators themselves, etc). For the research to be useful the choices would need to be assessed in the context of, say, nature of manufacturing process, size of company, etc. Better still any research should be done in the context of demonstration sites where some form of experimental control can be applied. In other words there is scope for a sensible extension of some of the work started in recent ESPRIT projects (i.e. projects 1199 and 534).

Planning and Implementation Methodologies

This is really a continuation of control of skill-based systems. It would be useful to test out the validity of methodologies such as those proposed by Nadler (1987). He has developed a set of procedures to bridge the gaps of understanding of how to plan, design and implement manufacturing systems. He argues that methodology is necessary to handle continuing change. It would be valuable for engineers and designers to test the Nadler model across a range of processes and industries. Is the model sufficiently robust, does it provide helpful insights on a quick enough time scale, is it easy to use, etc.?

Measures of Individual Discretion

A key consideration in designing and operating skill-based systems is the extent to which the operators can use discretion. Measures of discretion (e.g. level of decision-making) could prove useful in comparing skill-based systems and in assessing the balance between technology and human inputs. For example is a good system one which allows an operator to make a decision at the middle management level once per week but for the rest of the time the decision-making is at the semi-skilled level? Or is it better to devise systems which oblige the operators to use middle-management or supervisor-level decision levels constantly? If the latter, is it feasible and cost-effective? The use of decision band theory (Paterson 1977) could form a basis for such analyses.

Payment Systems

Novel payment systems could prove necessary for success in operating skill-based systems. Presumably quality of product would be an important element. Level of decision-making (and frequency) might be another. In developing appropriate payment schemes the comprehensive nature of the work of the operator would need to be included.

Maintenance Management

The role of the maintenance function is crucial in a technocentric system. It will also be of importance in skill-based work especially on a planned, life-cycle basis. How should maintenance be organised? Should it continue to be centralised (as in most factories) or is a localised task force approach better? Should planned inspections rather than preventive maintenance be used? How does condition monitoring impact on the role of maintenance management? The use of simulation could prove helpful to test various management strategies (see Husband 1983).

3.5.3 People

It is self-evident that people issues lie at the heart of skill-based technology. However it difficult to propose a wide range of research work which would prove to be of importance at the system design stage. There is much to be done after a number of skill-based systems are available for analysis. The measurement of job satisfaction in skill-based as against technocentric systems will be an essential consideration. Similarly, the comparative measurement of worker stress will be highly relevant. But these will be retrospective studies.

As noted earlier in this chapter the role of ergonomists and social scientists should include participation at the prospective, design stage alongside engineers and technologists. All research work in skill-based technology should only be funded on the condition that a balanced team of social scientists and technologists carries out the work.

A key prospective and people-related research topic relates to group cohesion. How can the chances of devising a CIM system which is skill-based and is managed by a set of operators who are well matched technically and socially be improved? Assessment, selection and training strategies will need to be developed to suit.

Training

The most important underlying issue is probably training. At national level, moves to curricula which emphasise learning by doing will continue to be important. Links between higher education institutions and industry will, naturally, also be significant.

At company level it will be necessary to develop methodologies for open learning. Research in this key area is likely to focus on the design of multi-media technologies; some work in the European Commission's DELTA programme could point the way.

The essential point to be made is that skill-based technology calls for training and re-training in the use and control of equipment requiring sensory and intellectual abilities. The design and management of relevant training programmes suitable, especially, for the SME is perhaps one of the highest priorities over the next 10-15 years.

CHAPTER 4

EUROPEAN RESEARCH IN ADVANCED MANUFACTURING

by

P T Kidd

Cheshire Henbury
Tamworth House
P O Box 103
Macclesfield SK11 8UW
United Kingdom

4.1 INTRODUCTION

It has been argued for several years that research in advanced manufacturing is technology led. Those who have practised technology led research have been dubbed by some people as technocentric or technology centred. It has been stated that the correct approach to advanced manufacturing should be an anthropocentric or human centred one.

Unfortunately however, the anthropocentric vs. technocentric debate has become polarised and over intellectualised. It is also a unnecessary debate because an increasing number of people recognise the importance of making use of unique human attributes such as creativity, skill. etc. Ayres (1990) for example, says:

"There is a controversy over whether the human centred approach is more effective than the machine centred approach ascribed to US firms where Taylorism was perhaps more entrenched. This is a false dichotomy, in as much as a computer integrated manufacturing (CIM) system can hardly operate without machines, nor can it function without humans. To achieve low defect rates, it remains necessary to eliminate humans from repetitive jobs where human error can lead to defective parts or assemblies. On the other hand, human talents are irreplaceable for non-routine functions like design, engineering, marketing, planning, diagnosis, trouble-shooting and general management."

This chapter has been written in the spirit of getting away from the polarised and over intellectualised debate, which seems to have become an end in itself. The aim of this chapter is simple: to suggest what research the European Commission should be addressing in the area of advanced manufacturing.

The argument is that market factors demand a new approach to advanced manufacturing and that this approach should be based on consideration of organisation, people and technology. Moreover, organisation, people and technology can offer manufacturing companies strategic advantages by virtue of a much improved capability to rapidly deal with increased complexity, without error.

This chapter will present a reference model for advanced manufacturing research for the 1990's and beyond, and will suggest changes that should be made to the ESPRIT-CIM and BRITE-EURAM research programmes.

4.2 THE NEW MARKET ENVIRONMENT - THE NEED FOR A CHANGED APPROACH

It is evident that market conditions have become more dynamic, more global and more customer driven. Product price is also no longer the main factor affecting business performance. Non-price competitive factors such as quality, design, delivery performance, product variety, and customer service are also important.

These market conditions will continue (Department of Trade and Industry 1989a) and an appropriate response is required from European manufacturing industry. Three potentially conflicting needs will have to be satisfied: reduced costs, improved quality and greater flexibility.

The Japanese have shown that high quality products can be manufactured without making a compromise between cost and quality. They are now expanding their product ranges. If successful they will provide customers with a large choice of competitively priced high quality products.

Without new technology no manufacturing company will be able to compete in these world markets, but European manufacturers must be sensible. New manufacturing technologies alone cannot provide the needed improvements in competitive performance. The problems of European manufacturing industry are complex and the solutions need a broad approach. There is no magical technological fix.

4.2.1 The Problems

Many technological developments have been influenced by the practice of replacing people with machines. In the past this has contributed to improved competitiveness. The people most affected by this have been those employed as direct labour.

In many manufacturing companies direct labour costs are now only a small percentage of total manufacturing costs (Department of Trade and Industry 1989b). Reducing direct labour costs therefore gives little scope for improving competitiveness. The response to the new market conditions needs a more sensible approach. Simple cost reduction exercises alone are not satisfactory in many cases and will not give the needed improvements in competitiveness.

Too often technology is seen as a panacea for the problems of manufacturing industry. This is natural because applying new technologies has worked in the past, and technology is obviously still important. New technology on its own however, is not enough.

Much of Europe's manufacturing industry has inappropriate organisational structures and outdated work practices. Technology is often used to resolve the problems created by these old fashioned organisations and work practices. For example, manufacturing throughput times can be reduced by applying new technologies. However, throughput time can also be shortened by making changes to the organisation and work practices. Often it is more appropriate to do this, than to apply new technology. Advanced manufacturing technologies should be used to reduce throughput times, but only after changes have been made to the organisation and the work practices.

Unfortunately, much of Europe's manufacturing industry still prefers to use organisational principles and work practices that were developed in the 19th century. Manufacturing is very hierarchical and centralised. Decisions are taken in the planning office and decision making is pushed up the hierarchy away from the shop floor. Five or six levels of management are also the norm in many companies, and manufacturing is divided into a large number of separate specialised functional units (e.g. turning shops, milling shops, quality control sections, etc.).

In the 1990's manufacturing companies should be using the organisational principles and work practices of the 1990's. Many are not and as a result they are putting themselves at a competitive disadvantage. The Japanese do not use 1890's techniques in their factories, and European industries must now modernise.

The organisational structures and work practices used in many European factories are old fashioned and inappropriate. They result in slow and inflexible factories. The development of advanced manufacturing technologies, such as CIM, has done nothing substantial to encourage the modernisation of these Victorian ideas. To remain competitive European manufacturing must consign these old fashioned ideas to the dustbin of history. They must adopt new techniques appropriate to the new market conditions.

4.2.2 The Response of the European Commission

There has been some criticism of the European Commission's research programmes in the area of advanced manufacturing. The research has been primarily technological, and the programmes and the European Commission have been dubbed as technology centred or technocentric.

The response of the European Commission to the needs of manufacturing industry seems to have been constrained by its own organisational structures. The European Commission, like many governmental organisations, is largely organised around functions. Probably as a result of this it does not have a well integrated research programme in advanced manufacturing and the research that it does finance is fragmented.

It is fragmented because it is split between at least five research programmes and three DGs. Advanced manufacturing research is undertaken within ESPRIT and within the BRITE-EURAM programme. The training and educational aspects of advanced manufacturing are covered by the COMETT programme, and these issues are also addressed within the DELTA programme. Innovation and technology transfer is addressed in the SPRINT programme. ESPRIT is administered by DG XIII and BRITE-EURAM by DG XII. The COMETT programme is administered by DG V. The DELTA programme is administered by another division within DG XIII, as is the case with the SPRINT programme.

Both ESPRIT and BRITE-EURAM are certainly deficient in their coverage of manufacturing. One research area which does not appear to be explicitly covered is manufacturing strategy, even though it has been shown that this is often more important to competitive manufacturing than new technology. No amount of new technology will make a company more competitive if the technology does not satisfy the needs of a business driven manufacturing strategy (Voss 1988, Department of Trade and Industry 1989b). Moreover, there appears to be no research within either programme that is addressing new management practices for advanced manufacturing.

Also, organisation and people aspects are at the moment inadequately addressed. Of the 123 CIM projects and exploratory actions funded by ESPRIT since the programme started, only two projects and one exploratory action have explicitly addressed human and organisational issues. These were projects 1199 (Human Centred CIM) and 534 (Development of a Flexible Automated Assembly Cell and Associated Human Factors Study). Only one of these projects (1199) was completed. The exploratory action is 5603 (Joint Technical and Organisational Design of CIM Systems for SME's). No BRITE-EURAM projects have explicitly addressed human and organisational issues.

This might be seen as evidence that there has been a lack of concern within these two programmes for the organisation and people issues. In some respects this is so. However, it should be remembered that these research programmes are industry driven. So if there is a lack of concern for organisation and people issues, the fault lies with industry as well as the European Commission.

It should be remembered that both ESPRIT and BRITE-EURAM were conceived as technological research programmes. Nevertheless, a number of other ESPRIT and BRITE-EURAM projects have been addressing organisation and people issues, albeit in a less obvious way than projects 534 and 1199 and exploratory action 5603.

ESPRIT project 2338 (Integrated Manufacturing Planning and Control System) has developed a decentralised system architecture which places more emphasis on short term shop floor scheduling and less emphasis on centralised scheduling of every resource at every moment of time. The short term scheduling can therefore be undertaken by semi-autonomous work groups. The system architecture being developed in this project resembles that developed by BICC Technologies as part of ESPRIT project 1199. ESPRIT project 2415 (Distributed manufacturing Planning and Control) is also addressing the development of similar systems.

ESPRIT project 5564 (Integrated Design and Evaluation of Assembly Lines within CIM) focuses on a number of assembly line design issues, including ergonomics and human factors.

BRITE-EURAM project 1381 (Interactive Knowledge Based Shop Floor Control System in a Small Manufacturing Enterprise Environment) is worthy of note. This project is concerned with the development of shop floor systems to support control and decision making by shop floor personnel. It is not a project concerned with automating the scheduling task. Rather it is a project that is addressing the development of a decision support system which leaves room for the exercise of the skills and judgement of the user. This type of project is compatible with the concept of making better use of the skills of shop floor employees, a philosophy that forms a central theme of ESPRIT project 1199.

The work undertaken in ESPRIT project 1199 is being continued in BRITE-EURAM project 3302 (Decision Support Systems for Production Island Based CIM for SME's). This project is concerned with developing decision support systems specifically for skilled shop floor workers.

BRITE-EURAM project 3345 (Development and Evaluation of Technologies as Support for Flexible Production Groups in the Clothing Industry), is another relevant project. This is concerned with developing technologies (sewing machines, automats, transport equipment, information and planning systems, etc.) to support semi-autonomous work groups.

Within the area of ESPRIT Basic Research Actions there is action 3143 (Factory of the Future Production Theory), which is developing a designer's workbench for the development of CIM in production systems. Organisation and people issues form an important part of this project.

It is also worth mentioning that in 1985, ESPRIT CIM-Europe established a special interest group (SIG) concerned with organisation and people issues in CIM, and that this SIG is one of the more active SIG's within CIM-Europe. Also, every CIM-Europe conference has had one session in which organisation, people and management issues were addressed.

The problem is not one of convincing the European Commission of the need to address a broader range of issues. It is more a question of providing advice on whether what is currently being done is adequate and whether the right topics are being addressed. Just because the European Commission funds projects in which organisation and people issues are addressed, does not imply that the right sort of work is being undertaken. Nor does it imply that enough attention is being paid to these issues.

4.3 THE WAY FORWARD

Manufacturing is not just a technical activity. People are also involved. The factory and the company needs the right sort of organisational structure. Human, technical and financial resources need to be managed in an appropriate way. When new technologies, new organisation and new work practices are introduced, the changes must be managed effectively. Change management is therefore required. New technologies, new organisations and new work practices also need new accounting procedures and financial appraisal methods. Company training schemes have to be developed. Business and manufacturing strategies have to be devised. And so on. These diverse activities all make an impact on business performance.

In most European manufacturing companies there is room for improvement and development in all these areas. There is also a need for research. Moreover, many of these activities are interrelated and cannot be treated in isolation. But this is exactly what is happening. What is needed is a research action in advanced manufacturing. An action that will address manufacturing as a whole. An action that will approach the issues in an interdisciplinary manner. An action that is broadly based. An action that will give manufacturing industry what it needs to compete in world markets.

4.3.1 Anthropocentric or Technocentric Research?

It has been suggested in several quarters that advanced manufacturing is technology led. This view now seems to be more widely accepted, and at the moment the policy of technology push which characterised many research programmes during the 1980's is very much out of favour. This can be seen very clearly in the UK, where the present emphasis of the UK Government's Department of Trade and Industry (DTI) is on management competence and manufacturing strategy. Technology is still encouraged, but only if there are good business reasons for its implementation. The important of organisation and people issues has also been recognised and the DTI is in the preliminary stages of preparing an awareness and research programme in this area.

In some quarters the technology led nature of research in advanced manufacturing has been given the label technocentric or technology centred thinking. It has been proposed that what is needed is an anthropocentric or human centred approach.

Some of the proponents of the human centred approach however, seem to experience sever difficulties in defining what the term means. This impression is reinforced by the content of some of the published literature on the subject. One clear message that emanates from some of these people, is that the human centred approach is the opposite of so called technology centred thinking. The anthropocentric approach is not the opposite of the technocentric approach, and should not be regarded as so. However, neither is it ergonomics or human factors engineering.

The anthropocentric approach has been exemplified by BICC Technologies' Manufacturing Systems Group. Although BICC Technologies have called their system human centred (Hamlin 1989, Ainger 1990), it is quite apparent that it is not based on any black and white analysis. The system design is based on modern organisational concepts and work practices. The technology has been developed to fit the organisation and the work practices. Instead of just using technology to improve business performance, organisational innovation and changed work practices have also been used. The role of the shop floor employees has been expanded and technology has been used to support all these changes. This is not human centred manufacturing but a sensible and balanced use of organisation, people and technology (Ainger 1990, Kidd 1990e). It is good engineering.

Balance should form the basis for a new research action. The aim should not be to shift from technology led research to human centred research. Over prescriptive approaches should be avoided. There is no one best human centred way. What is needed is a balanced approach: one that takes account of organisation, people and technology. Technologists should be encouraged to take a broader view of manufacturing, seeking the right mix, the right balance, for each problem that they address.

The important point is that a variety of research needs to be pursued. There is a need for business led research projects, but there is also a need for more strategic research with less emphasis on solving immediate problems and more on developing speculative techniques that may be adapted and applied to problems in the future. Likewise, there is still a need to invest in purely technological research, but there is also a need to undertake research based on an interdisciplinary approach to technological development.

ESPRIT and BRITE-EURAM are primarily technological research programmes. Whilst there are more projects addressing organisation and people issues than many people believe, there is at the moment an imbalance between technology and the organisation and people issues. The two ESPRIT-CIM research projects that have explicitly addressed the three areas, 1199 and 534, have also largely been multidisciplinary projects. The current situation is depicted in Figure 4.1.

What is needed is an interdisciplinary approach because there are areas that lie between disciplines that must be addressed. The imbalance between technical research and the coverage of the organisational and people issues must also be redressed. What is needed is a more balanced interdisciplinary approach. The desired situation in depicted in Figure 4.2. This figure does not suggest that organisation, people and technology issues need to be given equal financial resources, but that something should be done to redress the over emphasis on technology and the neglect of the organisation and people areas.

Imbalanced & Multidisciplinary

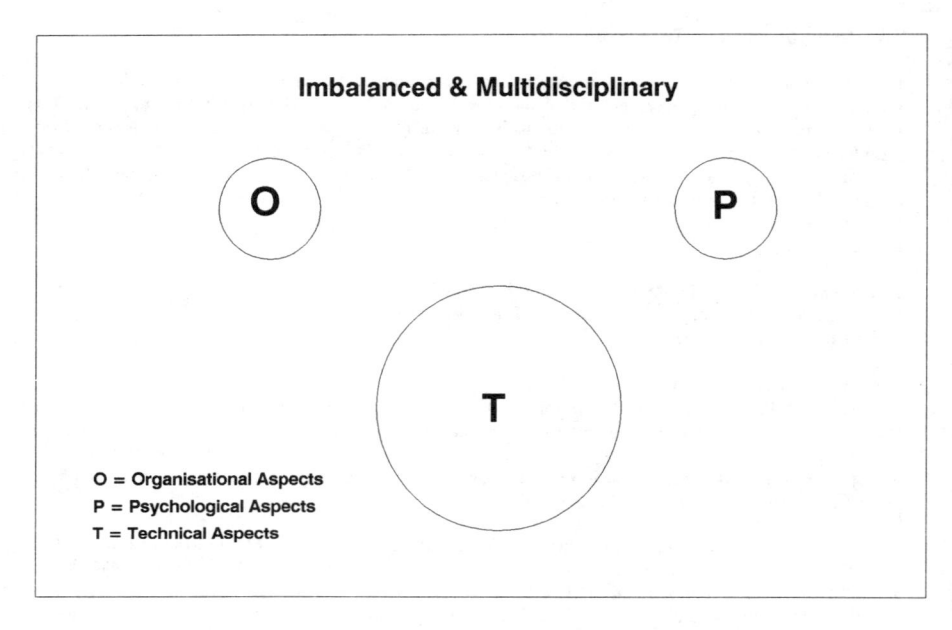

O = Organisational Aspects
P = Psychological Aspects
T = Technical Aspects

Figure 4.1: Research in Advanced Manufacturing - The Current Situation

Balanced & Interdisciplinary

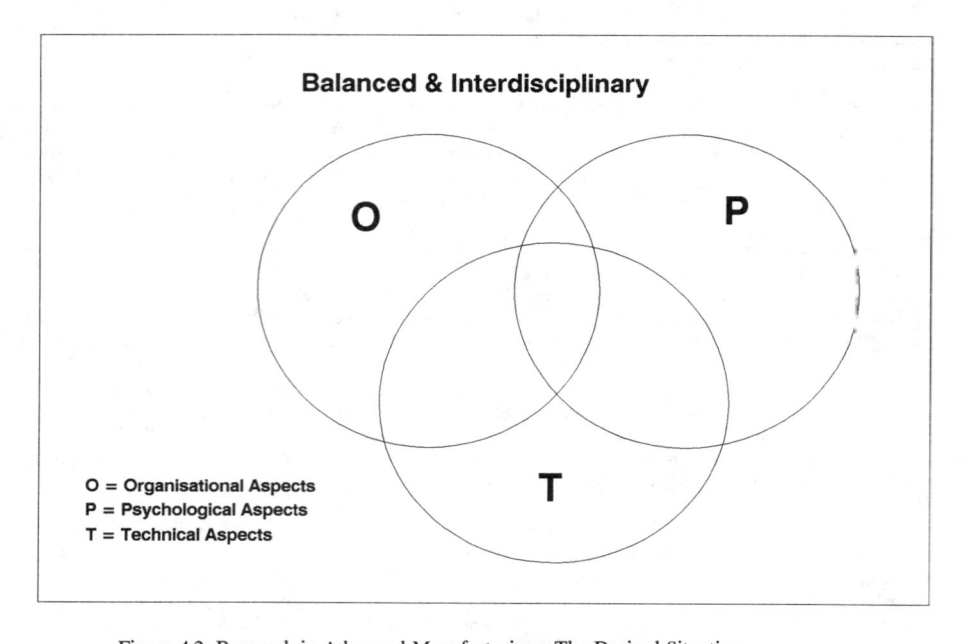

O = Organisational Aspects
P = Psychological Aspects
T = Technical Aspects

Figure 4.2: Research in Advanced Manufacturing - The Desired Situation

4.3.2 A New Approach to Technology

A different approach towards the application and use of technology is also needed. Advanced technologies need to be used to support people and the organisation. In many areas there is scope to develop skill supporting technologies. The idea of developing technologies to replace human skills is appropriate in some circumstances, but more imaginative use of technology is also needed. Technologies need to be developed that support the jobs that people have to perform. Technology should also allow people to use their creativity and skills in order that they can, for example, contribute to continuing improvements in products and processes, or assist with the management of complexity, etc.

This suggests that a different type of technology must be developed. For example, many expert systems have been developed to automate work. These systems reproduce expert actions, and while in theory it is possible to override or ignore them, what is required is a different technology.

This does not mean that developments in Artificial Intelligence (AI) have to be rejected. Rather it suggests that technologists must begin to take a broader view of the development and use of new technologies. An expert system that replicates human actions is firmly linked with the tradition of creeping automation. This is a process in which human work is gradually taken over by machines. The work that cannot be automated determines the users' tasks. There is room for other approaches. A more sophisticated and intelligent relationship between user and machine must be developed.

First there is a need to realise that it is unhelpful to talk about AI. This term is misleading and serves to focus attention on how to mimic human intelligence. All AI has to offer are computer programs. It would be more correct to talk of advanced computational techniques. Once this is realised then a little bit of imagination is also needed to develop a different type of technology, along with a willingness to think more broadly. At the moment it seems that both the imagination and the willingness are in short supply.

Technologists must appreciate that automation is not always the best solution. For example, advanced computational techniques can be used to provide knowledge-based systems that will advise rather than decide. It is often not necessary or desirable that the computer should solve a problem. What can be done however is to help the user to solve problems, say, by predicting the results of decisions, or by undertaking tasks that humans find difficult. It is important however, that the user should be in control.

The following serves as an example of what is proposed (Rosenbrock 1989, p 181):

Computer: A collision between the tool and the workpiece is predicted. Are you sure that the next move is safe?

User: Why collision?

Computer: Envelope of workpiece intersects envelope of tool at 35 percent motion of robot.

User: Show me.

Computer: (graphic display)

User: Envelopes are conservative. Move is safe.

Computer: OK. Suggest that you run it slowly first time, with your finger on the stop button.

User: OK. Go.

This type of dialogue is not easy to achieve at the moment. The example however, illustrates the direction in which research could be directed. What is needed is decision support, not automated decision making. Advanced computational techniques should not be used in a way that replicates what people can already do, or in a way that simply tells them what they already know. Instead, these new technologies should be used to advise the user about things he is unsure of, or which he does not know about, or to remind him of the consequences of his decisions, or to solve problems that cannot be solved using conventional algorithmic techniques or by people (e.g. scheduling tasks based on the travelling salesman problem).

In short, technologists should stop trying to remove the human from many types of work situations. Attempts to achieve this aim are rarely successful, often fail to take account of whether it is necessary, and invariably ignore the effect on the motivation of the people who will have to use the systems. The need to achieve greater flexibility in manufacturing while at the same time improving quality and reducing costs, suggest that manufacturing systems need to be designed with the aim of making human skills, judgement and experience more productive and more effective. The need to involve shop floor people in continuing improvements implies that technology should be designed in a way that results in improved motivation of the people who will use the systems. Technologically induced demotivation should be avoided through more broadly based design considerations.

4.3.3 A Reference Model for Advanced Manufacturing Research in the 1990's

Organisation, people and technology will form the basis of advanced manufacturing in the 1990's and beyond. Technology alone will not provide improved competitiveness. Human competence will play an important role in advanced manufacturing, and research programmes such as ESPRIT and BRITE-EURAM need a new focus.

It is necessary here to stress that what follows is not a prescriptive framework for research in the area of advanced manufacturing, nor is it intended to be a prescriptive solution to the various problems that beset manufacturing industry. It should be considered as a general reference model that provides a guide to the development of research programmes, projects and the design of advanced manufacturing systems.

The requirement for flexibility, adaptation, improved responsiveness, and the need to motivate people and to make better use of their skills, judgement and experience all suggest that organisations, work practices and technologies need to be developed in a way that will allow highly trained people, at all levels in the company, to adapt their work strategies to the variety of situations that they will have to face. This implies that organisations, work practices and technologies will have to be developed as open systems.

An open system allows people a large degree of freedom to define the mode of operation of the system and the form of interaction with the system and its environment. The term implies a system which is flexible. At the moment the term is very much associated in manufacturing with system architectures based on the International Standards Organisation Open Systems Interconnection (ISO-OSI) model. The concept of an open system is also used in management science however, to describe an organisational structure that takes into account and responds to the environment. The idea can however be given a much broader interpretation. It can be applied not only to system architectures and organisational structures, but also to work practices, human-computer interfaces and the relationship between system users and technologies such as shop floor scheduling and control systems, decision support systems, etc. (Kidd 1990b, 1990c, 1991b).

There are many possible new management perspectives. Peters and Waterman (1982) have termed one possibility, the open system, social actor approach, which recognises the social and open nature of organisations. In other words, the organisation must take into account and respond to the environment (open systems) and decisions must be taken on the basis of the dynamics that affect people working in groups (social actor).

To do this we need to create a new organisational model that will not only be effective and responsive, but will take into account peoples need for motivation. This 1990's model of the organisation is based on:

. a flat organisational hierarchy;

. a cell-based factory;

. decentralisation of decision making and control;

- increased competence of shop floor people;

- multiskilled employees;

- team working;

- empowering of people on the shop floor;

- skill supporting technologies;

- continuing improvement involving all employees;

Research in advanced manufacturing technology, where appropriate, should be based on an interdisciplinary approach. The technology should be designed to take account of the organisation and people considerations as illustrated in Figure 4.3 (Kidd 1991b). This diagram does not suggest that organisation and people should remain unaffected by technology. The organisation and the people may need to adapt to new technology, but technological development should take account of the desired organisational structure and the needs (e.g. psychological) of the people who will have to use it.

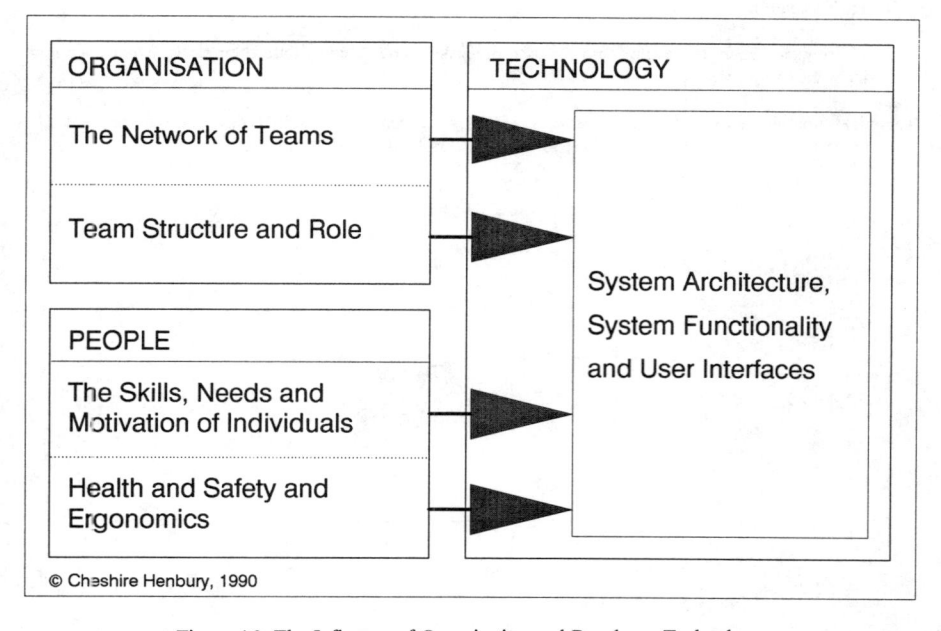

```
┌─────────────────────────────────────────────────────────────┐
│  ORGANISATION              TECHNOLOGY                       │
│  ┌──────────────────────┐                                   │
│  │ The Network of Teams │───▶┌────────────────────────────┐ │
│  │                      │    │                            │ │
│  ├──────────────────────┤    │                            │ │
│  │ Team Structure and   │───▶│                            │ │
│  │ Role                 │    │                            │ │
│  └──────────────────────┘    │  System Architecture,      │ │
│                              │  System Functionality      │ │
│  PEOPLE                      │  and User Interfaces       │ │
│  ┌──────────────────────┐    │                            │ │
│  │ The Skills, Needs    │───▶│                            │ │
│  │ and Motivation of    │    │                            │ │
│  │ Individuals          │    │                            │ │
│  ├──────────────────────┤    │                            │ │
│  │ Health and Safety    │───▶│                            │ │
│  │ and Ergonomics       │    │                            │ │
│  └──────────────────────┘    └────────────────────────────┘ │
│  © Cheshire Henbury, 1990                                   │
└─────────────────────────────────────────────────────────────┘
```

Figure 4.3: The Influence of Organisation and People on Technology

What is needed in the sphere of technological development is a new relationship between user and computer: an intelligent relationship between computers and intelligent people.

It has already been mentioned that traditional thinking is often based on the view that the user's role is to compensate for the inadequacies of the computer. The implications of this is that people have to intervene in the system operation. People are still needed.

Research programmes should now focus more on the principle that the user's role is not just to intervene but to be involved. This demands that people be viewed as desirable; the emphasis should be upon 'should be needed', rather than 'still needed'.

The difference between these two design perspectives is important and needs to be clearly understood. The former views people as complementary to the technology, the latter regards people as a necessity. The first encompasses the second, but not visa versa (Kidd 1988, 1989, 1990d).

Instead of designing technologies that result in the need to force square pegs into round holes, as depicted in Figure 4.4, a better approach would be to design the system to leave room for the exercise of existing skills, but also to allow these skills to evolve into new skills. This is illustrated in Figure 4.5. Instead of forcing a step change on the user, as illustrated in Figure 4.6a, there is room for a gradual development of the user's skills as illustrated in Figure 4.6b (Kidd 1991a).

The aim should not be to fossilise outdated techniques, but to:

. ease the transition from old to new working methods;

. create a flexible system which will allow skilled users to develop working methods that are appropriate to each situation;

. leave room for users to develop and practice their skills and to contribute their skills, experience and judgement to the work process.

Technical functionality should not therefore be king. User acceptance, useability, user motivation, and other user needs should play an important part in future technological developments.

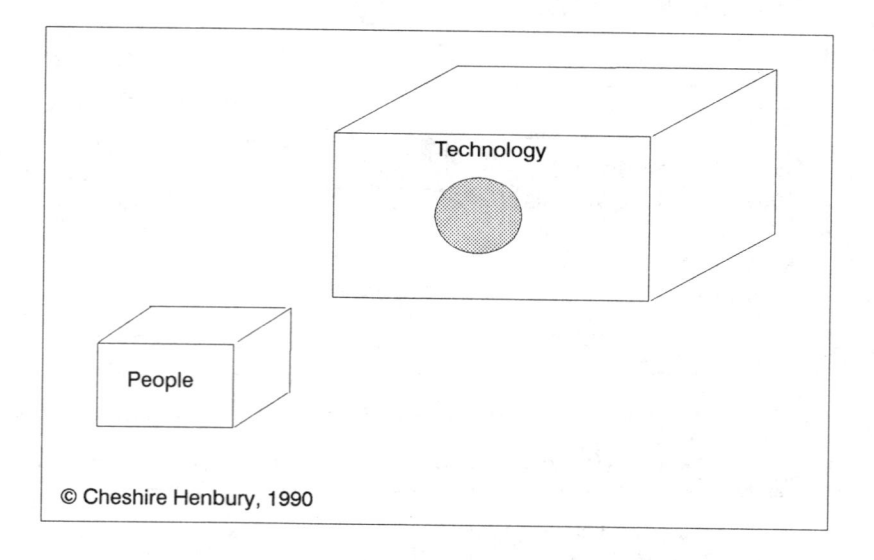

Figure 4.4: The Technologist's Approach to Change Management

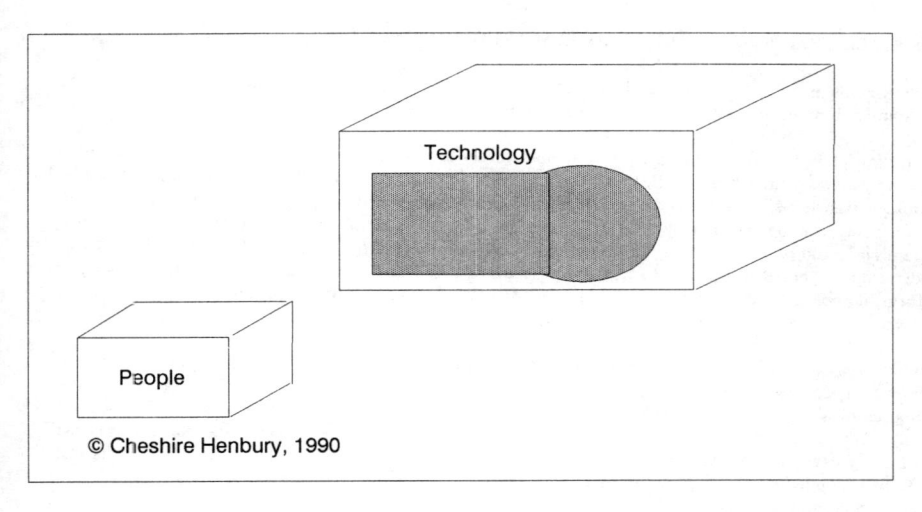

Figure 4.5: Change Management - The Unexpected Solution

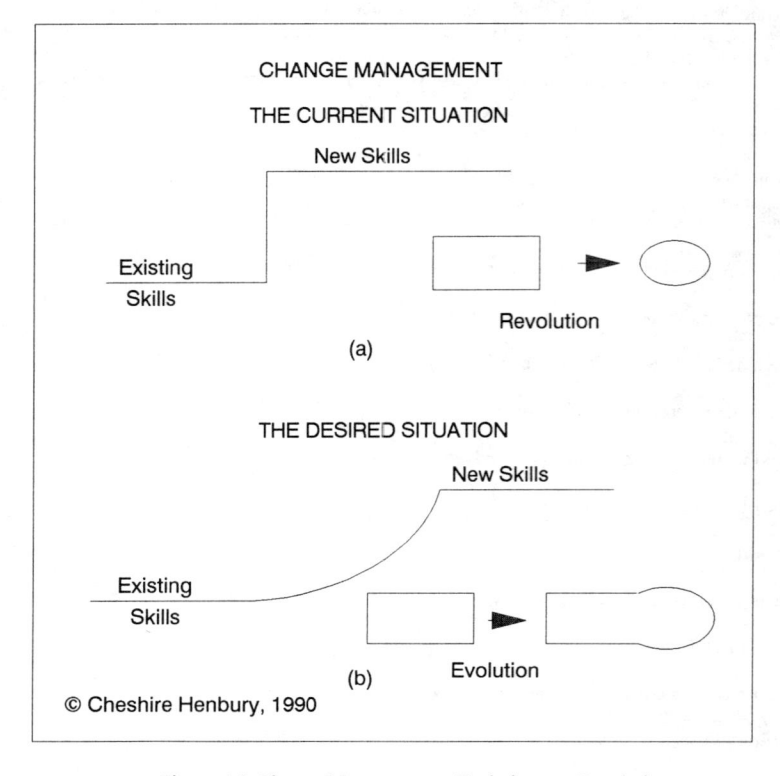

Figure 4.6: Change Management - Evolution not Revolution

4.4 DETAILED PROPOSALS FOR A NEW RESEARCH ACTION

The suggestion is to create a research action in advanced manufacturing, building on exiting research programmes in numerous DGs, and creating a new research programme to fill in the gaps.

The starting point for research in advanced manufacturing technology must therefore be existing research programmes. This primarily means ESPRIT-CIM and the relevant parts of BRITE-EURAM. Innovation and technology transfer should be addressed by SPRINT. Research in the area of training for advanced manufacturing can be covered by COMETT and DELTA. Any other areas not covered by these five programmes could be covered by a sixth programme specially created for the purpose. Thus ESPRIT CIM, the relevant parts of BRITE-EURAM, SPRINT, COMETT and DELTA, and this sixth programme, together will form the needed European research action in advanced manufacturing, which can be coordinated by a task force drawn up from Commission staff from the DGs involved in the existing programmes.

Given the constraints resulting from the European Commission structure and the desperately important need to adopt a broad cross functional approach to advanced manufacturing, a research action that crosses the boundaries of a number of existing research programmes and DGs is the only way forward. This will be difficult and troublesome to manage and to coordinate, but it is the only way forward that makes any sense given the constraints. Care will have to be exercised in the management of the task force, and efforts will have to be expended on creating a team that can overcome the bad effects of loyalties to DGs, divisions and research programmes.

It is important however, that the action be an interdisciplinary one and not multidisciplinary. Thus, for example, questions of user training, technology transfer, motivation, etc. must be considered in the development phase and should shape the technology. These issues should be integrated into technological research, and not just left for someone else to deal with after the technology has been developed.

The objectives of this new action should be to:

. Assist European manufacturing industry to become more competitive;

. Modernise the technology, organisation, and work practices used by European manufacturing industry;

. Promote European industrial cooperation in precompetitive advanced manufacturing research;

. Develop an interdisciplinary approach to advanced manufacturing.

The research action should address three key themes:

. Advanced manufacturing organisation;

. Advanced manufacturing management and work practices;

. Advanced manufacturing technology.

It should cover:

. The organisation of the factory;

. Change management techniques;

. Advanced management and work practices;

. Application of social science;

. Business and manufacturing strategy;

. Interdisciplinary manufacturing systems design;

. Manufacturing accounting techniques;

. IT systems to support people and organisation;

. Technological research.

Some of the existing purely technical research will remain unaffected by the new action. Only those areas which need to be approached in an interdisciplinary way should be changed.

The workprogrammes of ESPRIT-CIM and BRITE-EURAM should be changed in a way that results in complementary activities within the two programmes. This can be achieved if ESPRIT-CIM focuses on more strategic issues and BRITE-EURAM focuses on more problem and business driven research. Overlap between the two programmes in inevitable, but should be seen as an advantage rather than a source of problems. Overlap ensures a smooth transition from strategic research to applied research and can provide a focus for transferring the results of strategic research into industry.

The changes that need to be made to the ESPRIT and BRITE-EURAM programmes are considered in the following sections. The 1989 ESPRIT-CIM and 1990 BRITE-EURAM workprogrammes will be used to illustrate these changes.

4.4.1 Suggested Revisions to the ESPRIT Workprogramme

The research within ESPRIT-CIM should concentrate on strategic issues for the longer term rather than attempting to satisfy the shorter term business needs of user companies. It should focus on helping IT vendors to create the products that will fit and support the new organisational structures and work practices, and provide users with the methods and tools that will be needed in the years ahead to implement integrated manufacturing systems.

Manufacturing Systems Architecture

A lot of effort has been expended by ESPRIT-CIM on the development of open systems approaches and CIM standards. This work should continue within the new programme, but the research should be more interdisciplinary and should be based on modern organisation structures and work practices.

The research should also recognise that the needs of SME's are sometimes quite different from those of large multinational companies. There should therefore be more emphasis on low cost systems and on creating migration paths from existing (often low cost) proprietary operating systems such as MSDOS, and network standards such as Ethernet, to emerging open systems standards. This type of research will also give ESPRIT-CIM a stake in more shorter term business and problem driven research to ensure wider dissemination and take up of strategic research results within European manufacturing industry. This type of work will also provide overlap with the BRITE-EURAM programme.

The research should address the growing importance of flatter hierarchies and cell-based factory organisation. It should seek to develop CIM system architectures that reflect these changes in organisation and develop understanding of the inter-relationship between organisational choice and system architectures. The architectural and communication implications of cell based organisations manned by semi-autonomous work groups, where decision making is devolved to the lowest possible level in the hierarchy, should be explored.

The enterprise modelling tools and techniques being developed by the CIM-OSA project should be reevaluated from a interdisciplinary perspective, and their potential as an organisational analysis tool, rather than an information system design tool should be investigated.

Research could be undertaken within two areas:

area 1. Interdisciplinary Development of CIM Open System Architectures and Communications.

area 2. Architectures and Communications for Small to Medium Size Companies.

Manufacturing Systems Design and Implementation

Manufacturing systems design and implementation is important and involves numerous interdisciplinary research issues. It is an area which must address manufacturing strategy, detailed systems design, and implementation. There is a need to address financial justification and appraisal techniques, accounting procedures, factory management practices, organisational principles, work practices, human factors issues, as well as technical design. Many of these activities can be supported by IT tools, and there is a need to develop comprehensive interdisciplinary design methods that cover the overall design process, from development of business strategy, through to the implementation of manufacturing systems.

Research could be undertaken within five areas:

area 1. Tools and Methods to Support Interdisciplinary Design.

area 2. Development of Social and Psychological Criteria for Manufacturing Systems Design.

area 3. Technical and Economic Performance Evaluation studies of New Organisational Principles.

area 4. Business and Manufacturing Strategy.

area 5. Advanced Manufacturing Organisation.

Product Design and Analysis Systems

There is a need to shorten product development lead times and to make design activities more responsive to changing market conditions and potential manufacturing problems. There is a need for greater cooperation between design and other functions such as sales and manufacturing. Organisational barriers need to be removed, and technology to support the creative aspects of design needs to be developed. The sensible application of advanced computational techniques needs to be given attention, with emphasis on using these technologies to support designers rather than to replicate the designer's expertise.

Research is needed in two areas:

area 1. IT Systems and Organisational Techniques to Support Collective and Individual Decision Making in Design, Including Techniques to Facilitate Cooperation Between Design and Shop Floor Personnel.

area 2. Applications of Advanced Computational Techniques in CAD.

Management and Control of Industrial Processes

Research in this area must address the difficult question of change management. European manufacturing industry will need to undertake some fundamental changes over the next ten years, and these changes must be managed properly. Innovations in organisation and work practices will also require new management techniques and information and control systems to support these new approaches.

Research is needed in three areas:

area 1. Management of Change.

area 2. Management Practices and Techniques.

area 3. Management Information and Control Systems for Production Island Based CIM.

Robotics and Shop Floor Systems

New organisations and work practices will need new shop floor technologies. There is a need to develop technologies that support human skills. The useability of shop floor systems is a neglected area that must be given attention. Technologies are needed that will help in change management by building on existing skills and allowing these to develop into new skills. The sensible application of advanced computational techniques needs to be given attention, for example by using these techniques in a decision support role rather than in a skill substituting way. There are opportunities to develop products from this research, that will give European manufacturers of shop floor and robotic systems a competitive edge over non European competitors. There is also an opportunity to provide products that fit the nature of European manufacturing industry which is largely made up of SMEs and a highly skilled workforce.

Research is needed in three areas:

area 1. Information, Control and Decision Support Systems.

area 2. Application of Advanced Computational Techniques.

area 3. Development of Adaptable and Natural Language Human-Computer Interfaces.

4.4.2 Suggested Revisions to the BRITE-EURAM Workprogramme

The BRITE-EURAM workprogramme is divided into four technical areas:

. Advanced Materials Technologies;

. Design Methodology and Assurance for Products and Processes;

. Application of Manufacturing Technologies;

. Technologies for Manufacturing Processes.

Within each of these four Technical Areas the European Commission identifies Priority Themes which proposals must address. Design Methodology and Assurance for Products and Processes and the Application of Manufacturing Technologies are the two technical areas most relevant to the issues considered in this chapter.

The European Commission's priorities in the area of Design Methodology and Assurance for Products and Processes, are design, quality management and process control, with attention being paid to methods for avoiding or minimising maintenance, forecasting breakdowns and evaluating cost effectiveness. In the area of Application of Manufacturing Technologies, the priorities are to fund work which will help manufacturing enterprises to reduce the product design cycle, total process time and throughput time. The application of process technology and procedures to ensure high quality and cost effectiveness of products and components is also considered important.

The focus of the BRITE-EURAM programme should remain on projects addressing well defined problems which are close to solution, but where further research is needed to solve the problem. Projects should be solicited that attempt to use organisation, people and technology to solve these well defined problems.

Both technical areas provide opportunities for making better use of the skills of the workforce. It is suggested therefore that the European Commission should address projects which focus on using the philosophy of continuing improvements in products and processes to achieve improved quality, etc. Projects should consider an appropriate organisational structure and work practices, and greater emphasis should be placed on making use of the skills of shop floor employees. The technology can then be developed as a supporting environment.

For example, statistical process control tools could be used as part of a supporting environment, but these tools would need to be tailored to the needs of shop floor users.

The results of a number of existing BRITE-EURAM projects may well provide the basis for further research projects, with emphasis being placed on tailoring the results to the needs of shop floor personnel.

It is therefore suggested that an appropriate research theme for BRITE-EURAM would be to undertake the development of workshop oriented tools specifically designed for the shop floor user, taking into account the desired organisational characteristics (for example decentralised product based manufacturing cells) and the new work practices, as well as the existing skills of these shop floor users. This workshop oriented philosophy could be applied to a wide range of systems, for example part program and tool management systems, condition monitoring and diagnostic systems, etc. This research theme would also allow results from a number of ESPRIT projects to be adapted and then transferred to SMEs in a number of industrial sectors.

4.4.3 Examples of Projects

The following project descriptions provide a few examples of the kind of work that could be undertaken within European Commission research programmes. All these projects should involve both social scientists and technologists.

Manufacturing Strategies for European SME's

The objective of this project would be to evaluate the full scope for involvement of shop floor personnel in advanced manufacturing systems and to establish the best mix of technology and people for European SME's.

The project would address a number of industrial sectors. Analysis of these sectors would seek to establish generic business, technological and organisational needs of small companies in these sectors. From the analysis the areas where human input and skill could be used to most benefit could then be specified.

The results of the analysis could be used to outline manufacturing strategies for small companies based upon an appropriate mix of organisation, people and technology. These strategies could then be used to influence future directions of European Commission research programmes. The results of the analysis could also be used to examine the deliverables from existing ESPRIT and BRITE-EURAM projects in order to establish the suitability of current technologies for these companies and manufacturing strategies.

Methods and Tools for Designing Manufacturing Systems

There is a need to undertake research that will identify the questions that senior managers should be asking about organisation, people and technology when developing manufacturing strategies. What questions should they be asking when developing their business strategy? What questions do they need to ask when undertaking a manufacturing audit? How should managers collect and process the data and information?

Methods and tools need to be developed to assist managers to develop manufacturing strategies based on organisation, people and technology. Action research methods should be employed to devise, test and revise these methods and tools.

Once a manufacturing strategy has been developed, the next step is normally to define the architecture of the information and control systems. This must meet the information and control needs of new organisational structures and work practices. There is a need to help engineers develop architectures that reflect the changed role of shop floor people. Possible tools include reference models and IDEF0, but further tools also need to be developed, for example to facilitate end user participation in design.

Workshop Oriented Programming Methods

Some work has already been undertaken on the development of workshop oriented programming tools for machine tools. This should be further developed and applied to other devices such as robots.

On the machine tool side there is a need to address programming for situations where the component geometry is transferred directly from the computer-aided design system. There is also a need to improve feedback to the user from the actual machining process. Can vibration measurements, heat sensing, vision systems, coordinate measuring systems, etc., be combined in a multi-sensor environment to increase the amount of feedback to the user in a way that is meaningful and compatible with human needs?

Can decision support systems be developed that will assist the users of machine tools and other equipment deal with the complexity that will arise from increased product variety? For example, can pattern recognition systems be developed that will help users recover from data bases part programs for editing?

Open Systems Human-Computer Interfaces

The objectives of this project would be to develop user interfaces for shop floor systems that would allow the user to set-up the interface to match personnel preferences and needs. The aims of the project would be to develop an interface which would allow the user to define the human-computer dialogue, the screen layout, interaction medium, etc.

Another important aspect of this kind of project is the development of natural language interfaces.

Team Structures for the New Factory Organisation Model

There is a need to undertake research to establish the structure of teams, for example those used in semi-autonomous manufacturing cells. What sort of patterns are needed and most effective in different situations? Possible structures include fully integrated teams which combine many separate functions, e.g. maintenance, quality and inspection, machine setting, etc., right through to simple teams based on horizontal job mobility, i.e. switching workers between jobs with a similar characteristics.

An important question is how to design a team structure? What factors need to be taken into account?

The Computer Aided Flexible Craftsman

Flatter hierarchies and decentralisation of decision making towards the shop floor implies increasing the competence of shop floor employees. Industry does not therefore need machine minders and single skilled craftsmen. The need is for multiskilled computer-aided flexible craftsmen. But how will industry make the conversion? What methods of training should be used: class room, or action learning, etc ? What is the role of IT in this training? What needs to be taught? Just technology, or technology and social skills for team working? There is therefore a need to develop training methods, and to address content, and means of dealing with a variety of shop floor people (older workers, under performers, etc.).

The Interdisciplinary Manufacturing Systems Engineer

Once organisation and people issues are brought into manufacturing systems design, new knowledge and new methods of working are needed. Most engineers and managers do not have the knowledge and skills to work effectively on interdisciplinary research and design projects involving organisation and people issues. The need is to develop training and education material and methods to broaden the knowledge and skills of engineers at all levels. There is a need to develop design team structures to support interdisciplinary design. What to teach and how to teach is an important question to be resolved. There is a need to cater for the retraining of engineers in industry, and also to reconsider the structure and content of undergraduate education in European universities and other institutes of higher education.

CHAPTER 5

MANUFACTURING TECHNOLOGY: AN ANTHROPOCENTRIC APPROACH

by

Professor Dr.-Ing. G Seliger

Institut für Werkzeugmaschinen und Fertigungstechnik
Technische Universität Berlin
Pascalstraße 8/9
D-1000 Berlin 10
Federal Republic Germany

5.1 INTRODUCTION

Heightening international competition, growing customer orientation and the ever increasing pace of innovation combine to form an enormous challenge to today's industry. Flexibility of production and high standards of quality will be increasingly important for commercial success. In order to meet these requirements it is necessary to utilise and support employee's skills. As a result the Tayloristic approach of rationalisation by division of labour has now reached its limits.

Furthermore, most industrialised countries have experienced a shift towards greater consciousness of the interaction between technology on the one hand, and the environment and society on the other. A corresponding shift in societal values away from traditional ones like prosperity, economy and functionality, towards new values like health, environmental quality and evolution of the personality, has led to strong public criticism being directed against conventional lines of technology development. In this context, the term Anthropocentric Technology evolved as a battle cry of the sociologists against the engineers whose thinking they considered technocentric, i.e. regarding technology as a purpose in itself.

5.2 A WORKABLE DEFINITION

Luckily, the period of confrontation between social and engineering sciences is over for several reasons, some of which have already been mentioned and others which will be outlined later. One result of the new consciousness of engineers is the German Engineers' Association's guideline VDI 3780 (VDI = Verein Deutscher Ingenieure): 'Recommendations for the Evaluation of Technology' (VDI 1989). The first parts of this guideline deal with basic concepts and value systems, and may be helpful in finding a workable definition of the term Anthropocentric Technologies.

Technical systems and processes are in a manifold of connections with other technical creations, with natural environment, with individuals, social groups and society as a whole. Consequently technology must not be considered as a purpose in itself but as a means for achieving specific goals. Goals are competing with each other if achieving one goal impairs achieving the other one. Means are instruments to achieve goals and can be goals themselves. Goals or means can be preferred to other goals or means. Criteria help in deciding on goals or means to be preferred. A scale can be used to quantify criteria.

The main criterion for selecting means is obviously their usefulness to achieve certain goals. However, means have to be evaluated with regard to all their potential consequences. Criteria for evaluation and selection of goals as well as for judgement on means can be gained referring to values. Values require validity and consent. They are the result of individual and social developments under natural, societal and cultural conditions. Consequently value systems change in the course of history, and they diverge in different cultures and social groups. Needs and wants can constitute values. They can be expressed by interests of individuals or groups. Interests are pursued with individual or group related power. Contrary interests can lead to conflicts. In a civilised society conflicts are carried out in a regulated way. Rules and regulations are socially obligatory with an inherent trend to standardisation.

The existence of technical means and their properties are based on human objectives, decisions and actions, each of them expressing values. The space for objectives, decisions and actions is limited by general frame conditions, namely natural conditions and socio-cultural conditions. These frame conditions reduce the set of thinkable technical possibilities to the set of executable ones. Changes in socio-cultural conditions can expand degrees of freedom of action and make natural potentials available. The selection among executable technical solutions is based on preferences depending on relatively stable individual dispositions. In this context, disposition means a readiness to act and react in a specific form and content of behaviour under the experience of actual conditions.

Individual dispositions are formed under the influence of

. individual forms of general needs for preserving and developing human life;

. perspectives and attitudes according to rules set by the respective cultural environment, religion and social class;

. personal experience and ideals.

Consequently values will influence technical goals and decisions via both general, socio-cultural frame conditions, and individual preferences. There is a close interaction between general frame conditions and individual preferences. They have a historical quality in the sense that they will change to a considerable extent in the course of time. This historical change of values can be recognised in changes of priorities and interpretation of values. Value systems determine technical developments and are reciprocally determined by them. Figure 5.1 describes the development and selection of technical possibilities influenced by general frame conditions and individual disposition.

The overall goal of any technical action should be to preserve and improve human life by developing and reasonably applying technical means. The engineers' task within the societal division of labour is to develop technical systems and guarantee their functionality. Resources, e.g. raw materials, energy, labour, time and capital, should be used economically to gain a maximum output with a minimum input. A technical system is not a purpose in itself but a means to achieve goals outside technology and economy. These type of goals are oriented to values like prosperity and welfare, health, security, environmental quality, individual development and quality of social life. Some of these goals and values are competing with each other, some are instrumental to each other. Technology evaluation is a means for visualising conflicts in goals as well as positive and negative effects of different technologies, and for estimating usefulness and risks of new technologies.

Figure 5.2 shows these values and a few important relations between them. The following is a selection of operational criteria for the values mentioned above:

. Functionality can be interpreted in the sense of usefulness; feasibility; efficacy; perfection, i.e. simpleness, robustness, accuracy, reliability, time of working life; technical efficiency i.e. efficient use of resources, productivity; etc.

. Economy can mean cost minimisation; profit maximisation; long range stability and growth of business; etc.

. Criteria for public welfare are ability to cover social requirements; quantitative and qualitative growth; international competitiveness; full employment; justice in distribution of goods; etc.

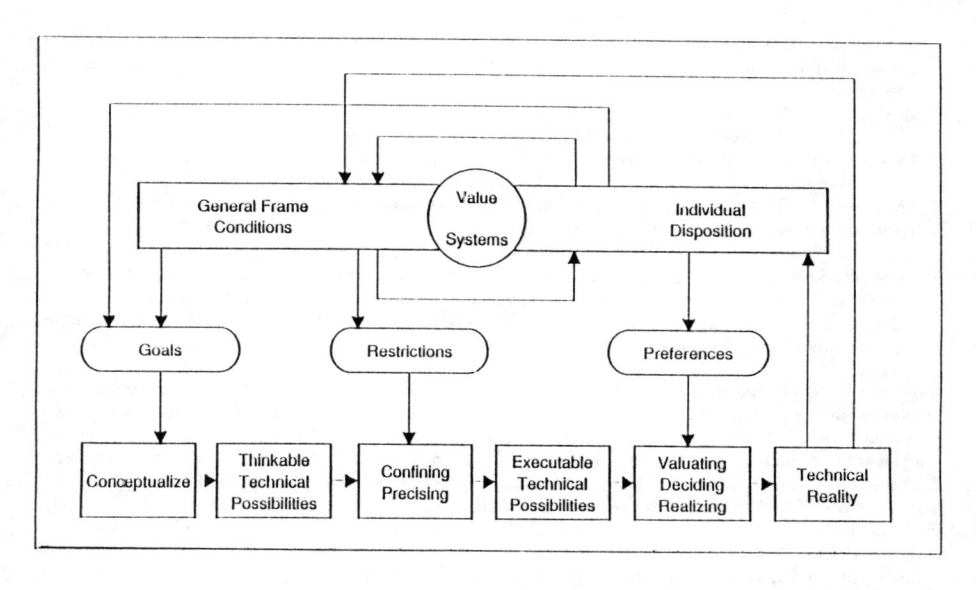

Figure 5.1: Development and Selection of Technical Possibilities Influenced by General Frame Conditions and Individual Dispositions

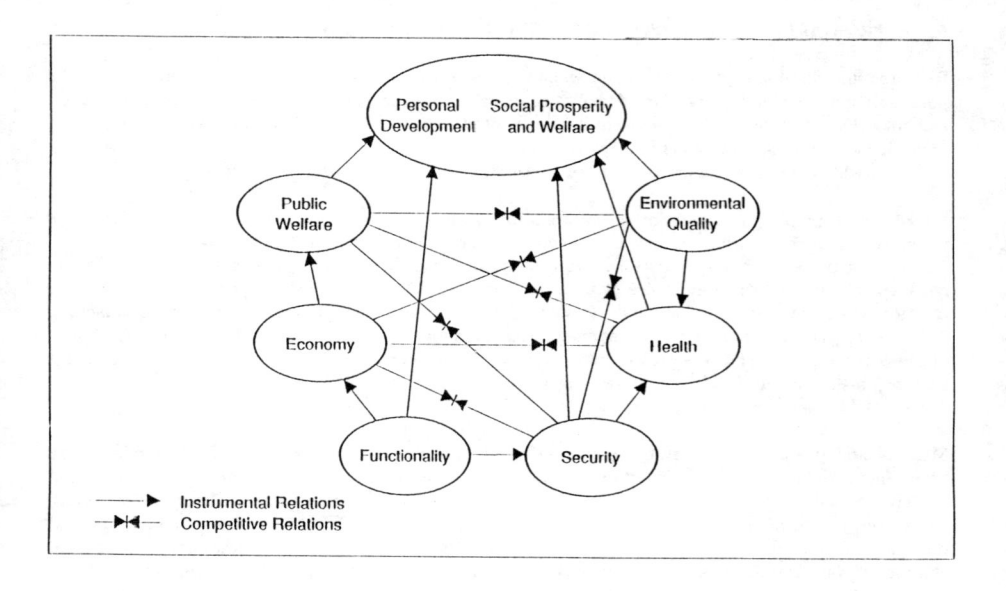

Figure 5.2: Values in Technical Action

69

- Security can be interpreted as freedom from physical injuries; preservation of human beings' and mankind's life; minimum risk (amount and probability of damage) in case of normal operation, failure and abuse; etc.

- Criteria for health would be physical and psychic comfort; long life; minimum direct or indirect health burdens at work and during leisure time; etc.

- Environmental quality could mean protection of species or landscapes; preservation of natural resources; reduced emissions and waste disposal; recycling; etc.

- Individual development and societal welfare can be interpreted in the sense of freedom of action; freedom of information and opinion; creativity; privacy; chances of participation; social contacts and acknowledgement; solidarity and cooperation; safety and security; cultural identity; social consent; order, stability and a level of standards; justice; etc.

It is Peter Brödner's merit of having drawn attention to some problems arising from a specific approach in manufacturing technology which he has called technocentric (Brödner 1985). This approach is characterised by an inclination to see automation as a purpose in itself, or to generally assign exaggerated values of functionality, economy and security to automated systems. Brödner has called for Anthropocentric Technologies in manufacturing, referring to basic characteristics of human work as defined by Hacker, Volpert and others. In the past the overly high valuation of the functionality criterion in manufacturing, induced by the imperative of faster - cheaper - more precise, has led to misguided developments of technology. These have resulted in the equally misguided conception that modern technology was inherently inhuman or even a threat to humanity. A more balanced system of values will enable us to develop technologies that will be less damaging to health and environment, more secure, will leave more opportunity for individual and societal development, yet will still be economic and thus assure prosperity. These future technologies can be summed up under Anthropocentric Technologies.

5.3 APPROACH FOR ANTHROPOCENTRIC TECHNOLOGY IN MANUFACTURING

Research and development of production technology always take place in a field of tension between the potentials of new technologies and the demands of applications in manufacturing. In consequence, production technology is not so much concerned with development of basic technologies but rather with applying them to production processes within the framework of natural and socio-cultural conditions. Basic innovations that have a considerable effect on production are information, material and process technology.

Information technology offers powerful tools for information, communication and documentation. Thus, the workforce in manufacturing can acquire a comprehensive knowledge about both product and process. Information becomes available in respectively adequate form, independent of time and place. This will enhance decision making competence at shop floor level and thus open up the opportunity to reintegrate functions that, due to the division of labour, were hitherto performed in different departments of a factory. This kind of job enrichment, possibly combined with some form of participation in the commercial success of the company will result in a greater awareness of each worker's personal contribution and, eventually, greater job satisfaction. Experiences of the Japanese who have advanced further along this path than many European companies are quite promising.

Material and process technology open up new possibilities of products and processes that protect the environment and improve utilisation of our natural resources. New materials permit improved efficiency and reduced emissions at the same time. New production processes allow for increased use of recycled materials, lower energy consumption and a reduction in waste and emissions. Application of innovative materials and processes is essential in order to keep up with the general demand for improved products on the one hand and the growing unwillingness to bear the environmental burden of industrial production on the other.

The following examples illustrate chances of Anthropocentric Technologies in manufacturing.

5.3.1 Factory Modelling

Factory Modelling is one important application of information technology. Essential reasons for unsatisfactory performance of production systems are (Grotrian and Seliger 1986, Wieneke-Toutaoui 1987):

- The functions of production equipment, data processing equipment and human workers are diverse and interact in a complex way which is often not readily apparent.

- The division of labour promotes one-sided system views.

- Knowledge about a given manufacturing system is rendered obsolete more rapidly by fast developing production technology. This makes thorough understanding of a system difficult simply due to lack of time.

- Increasing automation makes workers less familiar with production. Past experience may be lost. Also, the creativity that used to be stimulated by direct contact with a system is now suspended.

Therefore, information processing systems have been conceived that help the planner of a manufacturing system in the design of a satisfactory system, and afterwards assist the operator in its operation. As the complexity of a manufacturing system increases the number of design alternatives which have to be considered rises, thereby complicating design decisions. An integrated set of tools supports generation and evaluation of manufacturing system models as well as interactive design and optimisation. The evaluation of system performance (performance modelling) is supplemented by an economic assessment (cost modelling).

Functional abstraction produces a solution-independent functional model of a real or fictitious manufacturing system. Figure 5.3 shows how, without the support of functional description means, the available solution space for a specific problem is reduced by the experienced planner's prejudice. This is because very early in the planning process the planner forms a topological imagination of a possible solution, under the influence of past experience, incidental ideas and his creativity.

With integrated planning assistance (Figure 5.4) the solution space is much less restricted because the user can find, analyse and evaluate all possible solutions to the principal subfunctions of the system as well as their possible combinations. Furthermore, the quality of a solution is much less dependent on the experience of the planner. Scenarios of potential consequences provide a basis for decisions that hitherto were generally made by the educated guess. Support of the user's creativity is one important aspect of Anthropocentric Technologies, enhancement of decision making competence is another.

Figure 5.5 represents a possible system's architecture. Two principal functions constitute the kernel:

- model generation, and

- model evaluation.

Each function works on a common functional model of a manufacturing system which the user describes in terms of the Manufacturing Description Method (MDM). MDM is a formal specification language which permits the modelling of all production system activities, structuring of the system, and use of standard modelling functions. MDM consists of function primitives like, for instance, REST, MOVE, MAKE, VERIFY, and description rules for manufacturing systems. Both basic functions consist of several subfunctions according to a hierarchical system structure. The model generation function comprises structural planning, topological planning, sequential planning and allocation of resources, such as robots, machine tools, vehicles, personnel, etc. The model evaluation function consists of performance modelling and cost modelling.

The user builds up a simulation model from MDM primitives. The model allows for simulation runs with different parameter settings and provides performance and cost data. The simulation results may call for modifications in the design which have to be evaluated by further simulation runs. In this way the model can be interactively refined until the design objectives are met. Performance simulation supports the verification

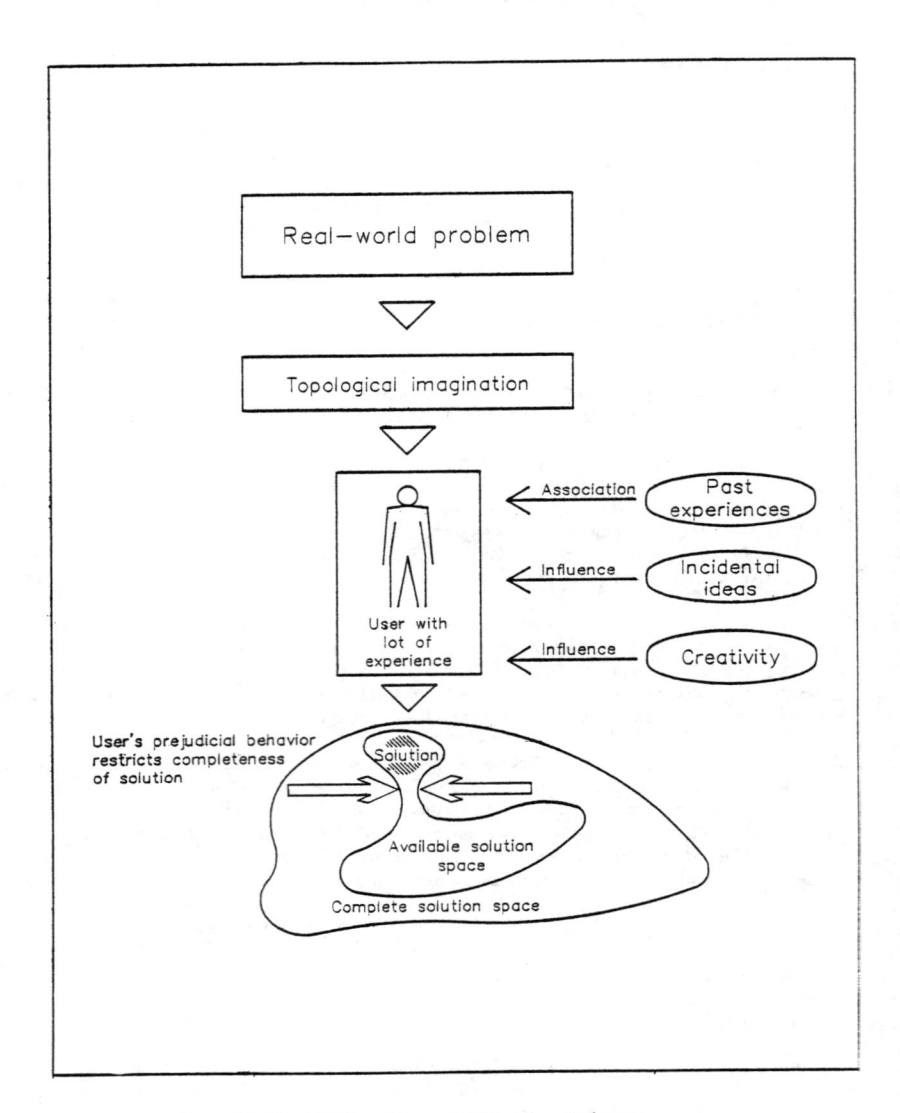

Figure 5.3: User Without Integrated Planning Assistance

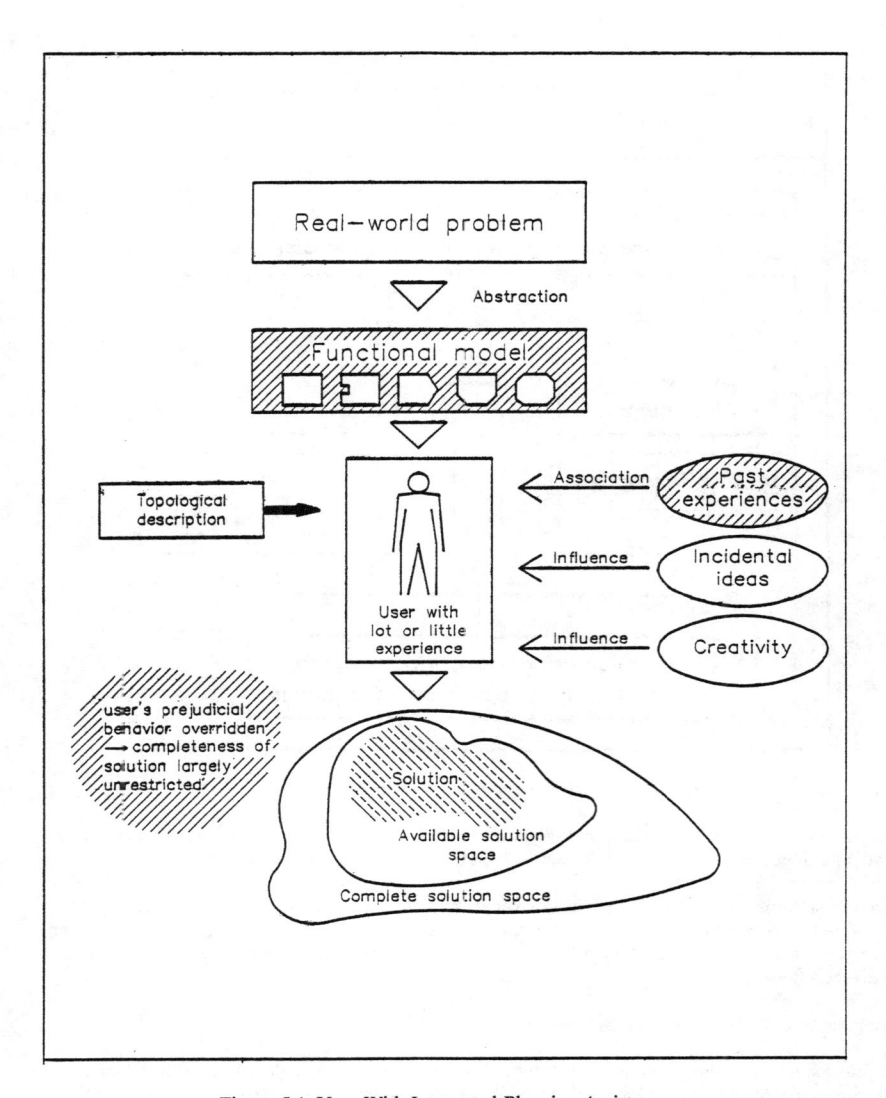

Figure 5.4: User With Integrated Planning Assistance

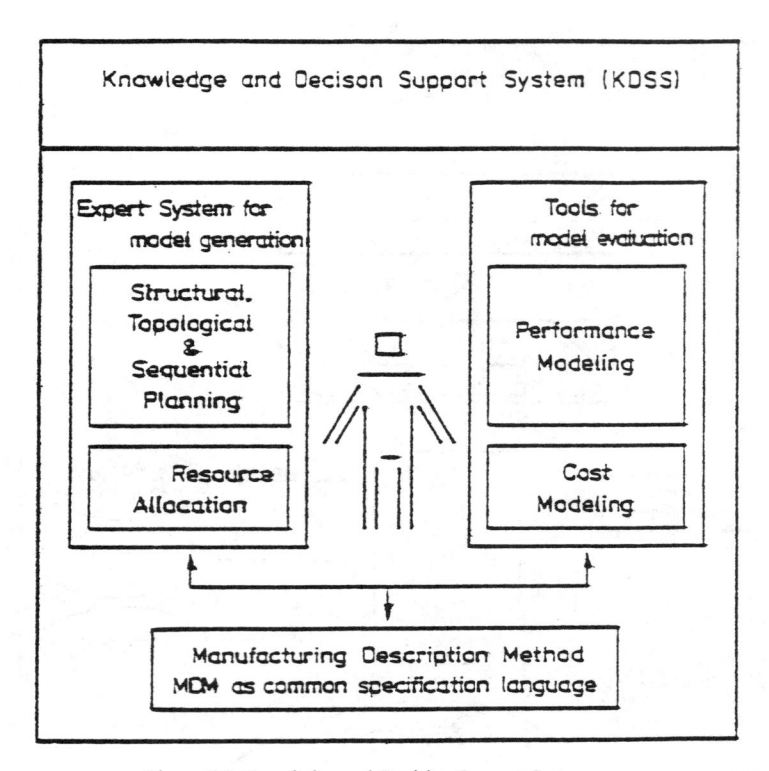

Figure 5.5: Knowledge and Decision Support System

of design parameters with respect to resource requirements. It can determine bottlenecks in a material flow, the impact of equipment breakdown, or the system behaviour with changed parameters.

After realisation the planning data and simulation capacity must be available to the system operator. They allow him to fully understand the system's functions, to optimise and, if necessary, to adapt them. Thus, even if a separated planning department still exists part of its planning and scheduling competence is delegated to the workshop floor.

5.3.2 Competence Oriented Workshop Scheduling

Another information technology tool is Competence Oriented Workshop Scheduling (COWS) (Spur et al. 1982). Decision making in manufacturing can be described as a system of superimposed control loops from the short-term operative process control via job scheduling to the long term product and investment planning. Whilst conventional computer based planning aids only support long term planning and general scheduling tasks, COWS permits computer aided disposition of facilities on the shop floor. This provides for a fast, flexible reaction to unforeseen events, such as tool or machine failure, employee illness or urgent orders. Such a transfer of scheduling competence to shop floor level calls for a comfortable man-machine interface, powerful means of description and access to planning information on the one hand, and machine status data on the other.

Scheduling tasks can be described in a problem oriented programming language which offers real time multi-tasking and portability. There are two types of data: basic data, such as product identification codes, working plans, or NC (Numerical Control) programs, and changing data like machine status or production programs which have to be updated at regular or irregular intervals. The system uses a standard DNC (Direct Numerical Control) interface for exchange of machine data.

Despite the efforts of Operations Research there is still no generally applicable algorithm for the disposition of facilities. In consequence, an interactive heuristic approach was followed. The actual status of, and feasible utilisation programs for, facilities are shown on a visual display and the shop foreman who uses the system decides on how to distribute the jobs among them. It is obvious that a good design of graphics displays and dialogue functions is of the utmost importance for the success of the system.

5.3.3 Rapid Prototyping

Rapid prototyping is another means of transferring competence to the shop floor. The early introduction of new and maybe not fully mature technology allows workshop personnel to express their views on it and participate in its perfection. If this approach is to be successful a certain amount of flexibility in both hardware and software is essential. One way to achieve software flexibility is the option of user-defined macros on computer numerical controls (CNC) which is already available from Japanese machine tool manufacturers. By defining a certain set of instructions as a macro which is then available at the fingertip, the operator can reconfigure the CNC for his needs.

5.3.4 Expert Systems for Diagnosis

Expert systems open up a great new potential of information, communication and documentation because they permit electronic processing of incomplete, insecure, or even conflicting data. Much of the knowledge humans gain from experience falls into this category. If we could use the experience of a maintenance expert, in detecting and rectifying faults, to qualify the system operator, we could again transfer competence to the shop floor. Seliger et al. (1989) introduce a knowledge based diagnostic system for automated assembly lines that is implemented on a micro computer using an expert system shell. A frame oriented knowledge base comprises knowledge about the assembly process, the assembled product and the assembly system. A rule base contains causal relations between symptoms and faults.

Starting out from a set of status data received from the assembly line controller the system tries to verify a fault by asking the operator for additional information. The likeliness of a certain fault is expressed by a confidence factor attributed to the respective rule. The confidence factors are automatically adapted to working experience by a statistics module. When the system has identified a fault it suggests how to repair it, or suggests that a maintenance expert should be called in. Justification and explanation modules are provided to make both the actions of the diagnostic system and the working of the assembly system understandable to the operator. Obviously the knowledge base and explanation facilities offered by such systems will also permit qualification of their users.

5.3.5 Training and Qualification Systems

Generally speaking, qualification is a keyword if we want to reduce vertical division of labour and transfer planning, scheduling and control competence to shop floor level. Purpose designed training systems allow for systematic training programmes. Advanced systems of this kind integrate video, graphics, text and sound. The progress through and in some cases even the sequence of the lessons is determined by the user's inputs. The output functions offered by state-of-the-art computer based training systems are sophisticated; user input, however, is still generally via keyboard, a rather clumsy method. This may make the system unattractive to the inexperienced user.

5.3.6 Work Organisation

What will work in the factory of the future be like? It will certainly be much different from today. Group work will be much more common. A few firms have already introduced group work in assembly lines. The continuing trend of automation will reduce the number of tasks that require manual labour, and in consequence a new form of group work will evolve. The flexible, automated factory of the future will be run by a system team with universal qualification (Figure 5.6). The members of this team will perform manual jobs as well as planning, scheduling and optimising procedures. The division between white collar and blue collar jobs is weakened. The team will be self-organising, autonomous and directly responsible to top level management. It will be supported by powerful computer based planning and control aids.

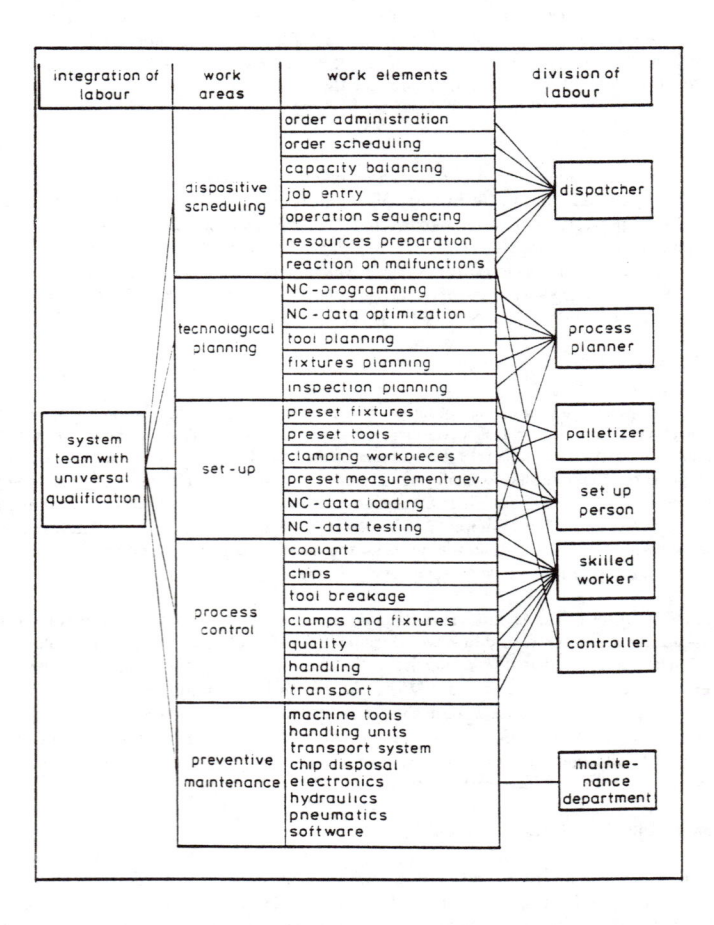

Figure 5.6: Design Alternatives for the Organisation of Work in Automated Flexible Manufacturing Systems

5.3.7 Preservation of Natural Resources

Work plays a very important role in the life of working people. A rather large amount of life is spent at work, and this argument alone justifies an effort to make work more attractive and satisfying. Luckily life is not work alone, so it would be unwise to restrict the meaning of the term Anthropocentric Technologies to the conditions of work. That would be a rather technocentric view. It is quite clear, for instance, that it is not possible to maintain the present standard of living unless natural resources are used much more efficiently. Despite some progress in recent years further advances in reducing energy and water consumption as well as waste and emissions of all kinds are necessary. Engineers will have to provide the new technologies to achieve this. Recycling must be introduced of the materials used in consumer goods. Other important aspects of Anthropocentric Technology, as defined above, that merit at least a mention are the use of regenerative energy sources and civil use of military technology.

5.4 ORGANISATIONAL AND ECONOMIC ASPECTS

The challenge of strong competition, high customer orientation and accelerating innovative pace can only be met by manufacturing systems that are both more flexible and more productive than their predecessors. Flexibility of machine tools, however, generally increases in the inverse ratio to their productivity. Consequently, the production system must be examined from a holistic point of view, and potentials for rationalisation identified.

5.4.1 Zero Reject Production

An enormous potential lies in the reject rate; 10-20 percent of an enterprise's turnover is wasted on rejects. Since usual rates of return are between one and five percent, addressing this problem is obviously attractive. To achieve Zero-Reject production each productive worker must have a sense of responsibility for the quality of his or her work. In the past vertical division of labour, in combination with automated machine tools, has often resulted in workers believing that their job was to run the machines, and whether the parts they turned out were good or not was quality control's concern. This is a folly, of course, that results in a high reject rate because the quality of a product is always determined by its design and the manufacturing process, no matter how efficient the quality control. It is quite clear that delegation of competence and responsibility for quality to the workshop will achieve significant cost savings. Improved information, communication and documentation will permit comprehensive testing, full process control and thus, higher valued goods manufactured at reduced cost.

5.4.2 Just-In-Time

A further reduction of costs is possible if the amount of storage can be minimised. This approach is generally known as Just-In-Time (JIT) manufacturing and is often understood to include Zero-Reject. In conventional manufacturing systems storage is necessary to allow for unforeseen events like urgent orders, or failure of a supplier to deliver. Since a flexible adaptation to such events is not possible, several days' supplies have to be stored to keep the production line running. If storage is to be done away with, then advanced information systems are needed which, for instance, will allow all departments within the factory, as well as external suppliers, full access to production planning data. There is also a need for flexible manufacturing and material flow systems and a highly competent, adaptable, motivated and self-organising workforce. Decision making must be delegated to the workshop. The calculative and operational costs of storage, especially of finished goods, make a dedicated effort worthwhile.

5.4.3 Qualification as an Asset

Ever shorter innovative cycles call for life-long learning. Instead of training a worker once and expecting him to do the same job for the rest of his life, it is necessary to retrain him or her for a new one every five years or so. How can it be done? First of all he or she must acquire and retain so called key qualifications. Basically this means the ability to learn. Any person who does monotonous or undemanding work over a long period of time will lose this ability. In order to retrain this person it is necessary to train him or her for learning first. Job enrichment can help a worker to retain key qualifications and thus reduce the effort necessary to acquire a new qualification. It is also necessary to maintain employees' interest in their jobs. Information technology and new organisational structures open up the possibility of machines and facilities that are designed to further qualify their users.

There is one other aspect to the issue of qualification. It is possible to distinguish between two different ways of developing automated manufacturing systems (Figure 5.7). Starting from the present Tayloristic workshop we see improvements in productivity and prosperity which in turn lead to a higher level of education and leisure pursuits. Industrial work will become unattractive to such an extent that a serious lack of competent skilled workers evolves. Now there are two ways to solve this problem: transfer competence to central information processors and leave an ever shrinking number of tasks to fewer and fewer unskilled manual workers, or improve man-machine interaction and make the factory job attractive again. The first way looks more promising on a short term basis owing to the immediate cost reduction. Despite short term success it eventually results in a loss of competitiveness owing to lack of creative competence of the human workforce. So, in the long run, the second way is more successful.

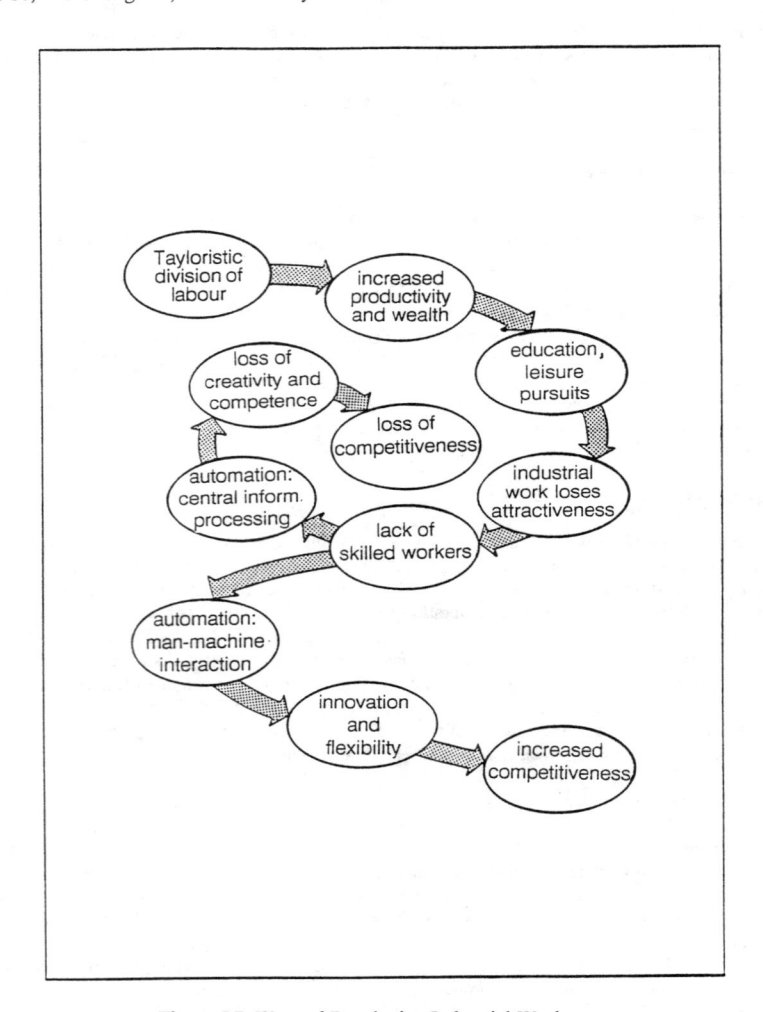

Figure 5.7: Ways of Developing Industrial Work

Figure 5.8 quantifies this effect by giving a formula for calculating productivity gains for each of the strategies. Strategy 1 uses automation to reduce dependence on a human workforce while strategy 2 uses automation as a means of increasing the creative and innovative potential of the enterprise. The high productivity gains that characterise the early stages of strategy 1 dwindle away with each step of the automation process. Contrary to this, the gains of strategy 2 are consistent, if slightly lower in the beginning. After four innovation cycles strategy 2 has overtaken strategy 1.

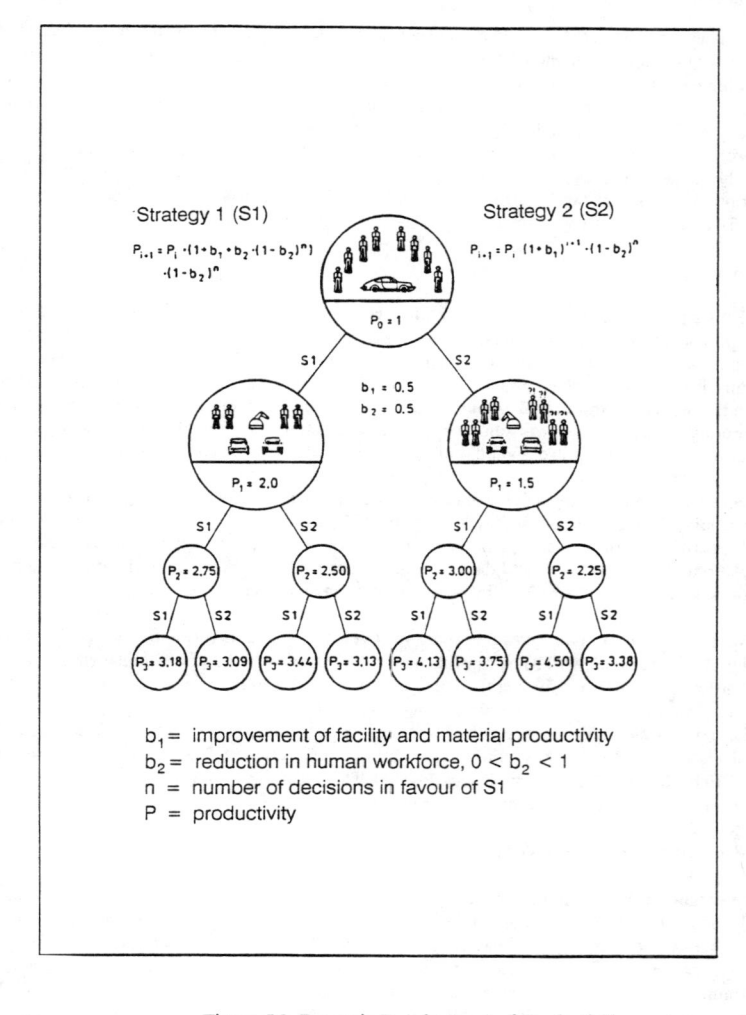

Figure 5.8: Dynamic Development of Productivity

5.4.4 One of a Kind Production

Another trend most threatening to Tayloristic manufacturing is rapidly increasing product variety. Today consumers expect high product quality, short delivery lead times and properties that exactly match their requirements. They are unwilling to pay for features they do not want but they are prepared to pay a higher price for a product that includes all the features they do want. This trend will eventually lead to One of a Kind Production (OKP) (see chapter 2). The task will be to develop technologies that permit manufacturing of the personalised consumer product with the efficiency of mass production. This approach is anthropocentric in itself because it makes custom made goods, hitherto handcrafted and offered only at forbidding prices, available to everyone. Increased customer satisfaction is certainly an anthropocentric value!

But OKP also implies a new production system. In order to achieve short delivery lead times and good value for money, Zero-Reject and JIT manufacturing are inevitable. Flexibility and adaptability requirements of OKP are much higher, though, than of JIT alone. To realise OKP the shop floor will have to be provided with full access to all data bases of the enterprise. Again, delegation of decision making competence to the shop floor is a keyword. Research and development, design and production departments will have to interact much more closely if a significant reduction of order lead time is to be secured. After implementation of JIT manufacturing the idea of JIT design is certainly in the air. This will involve CAD systems with far more powerful description, simulation and calculation means than is known today. And what is the business justification? It is very simple: if you cannot deliver you are out of business!

5.4.5 Management

The management structure of today's enterprises is characterised by a Tayloristic division of labour similar to the workshop. The partition of tasks tends to increase with the size of the enterprise. What the self employed has to do alone is performed in more than a dozen departments in a large company. The efficacy of such a structure is reciprocal to the amount of coordination and information exchange between partitions. Flexibility and adaptability call for a large amount of coordination and information exchange. Consequently, when a novel product is to be introduced some large companies establish a new division and shut down an established one rather than having it designed, built and marketed by an existing division.

Computer Integrated Manufacturing (CIM) has been seen as a means of increasing effectiveness and flexibility of the traditional management structure. The effort is quite hopeless, however, because information systems that support the existing management structure are not designed for cooperation. And even if the necessary Local Area Networks (LAN) and data interfaces were provided the amount of data exchange and job coordination would make this kind of CIM structure extremely expensive and inefficient.

Figure 5.6 shows how new information systems and a new management structure influence each other and eventually lead to integrated teamwork. This approach must be extended to the whole management. This will not only result in fewer departments within the company and thus a significant reduction in frictional loss, but also a smaller number of management levels owing to delegation of decision making competence to the basic level. There is considerable economy to be gained from reducing the middle management. The Japanese who have started on this way now have a ratio of indirectly productive to directly productive employees of 90:100, while the German average is 144:100. This means that Germany has 60 percent more office staff for every manufacturing worker than Japan!

5.4.6 Product Properties: Ease of Recycling

As stated above certain properties of the product can constitute anthropocentric values so it is necessary to analyse not only the manufacturing process and the factory organisation but also the product itself. Customer satisfaction has already been mentioned. Increasing concern for the environment will induce a demand for products that preserve resources and do as little damage to the environment as possible. But there is also an economic argument in favour of design for ease of recycling and especially ease of disassembly. If the different materials can easily and cheaply be separated, what used to be just scrap becomes a valuable (and well paid for) resource. Even now aluminium smelters are buying back 60 percent of their production in order to save the expensive and energy consuming smelting of bauxite.

5.5 COUNTERACTING FORCES

It is inevitable that changes of the scale and scope suggested have to overcome considerable counteracting forces. Very often the underlying reason is that people who were brought up in certain traditions have difficulty changing their views. 'Not invented here', 'we have always done it like that' and 'it is against company policy' are common expressions of this problem. Objective problems, traditional individual dispositions and institutional inflexibility are conservative forces. If the conflict between progressive and conservative forces is carried out openly, as it should be in a democratic society, it will eventually result in a rate of progress that is perceptible to everyone.

An objective problem is the expenditure necessary to introduce anthropocentric technologies. Thorough reorganisation of work and acquisition of the necessary technology will only be possible at a high cost. Half-hearted approaches may save money in a short term but will be less effective. Usually a company does not change the way it operates while it is doing well. When it is doing poorly it must improve efficiency and reduce costs in a very short time to survive. It will have no choice but to resort to strategy 1 (see Figure 5.8).

A problem of individual dispositions arises when workers used to a Tayloristic environment are suddenly called to take over control, or even planning responsibility. They are often content with executing other people's orders because that is what they are used to. This effect of the individual's socialisation is inevitable and limits the speed of change. The common idea of the class struggle between those who do the work and those who control (and exploit) them exacerbates this problem. On the other hand, the individual disposition of a member of the middle management which, under the proposed organisational structure, would largely be abolished, will not be favourable as well. It is necessary to be very careful not to demand too much. This kind of acceptance problem also occurs with respect to the product. For instance, people tend to regard recycled materials as second-rate which may result in firms keeping their use of recycled materials a secret.

Inflexibility of institutions will provide the most difficult obstacle, though. Most blue collar workers work to rigid job descriptions, or work rules which in some cases have legal character. If they are asked to perform non-regulated functions they have the right, and are in fact encouraged by their trade unions to refuse this particular job. Owing to the traditional partition between blue collar and white collar jobs, planning and control generally fall outside the tasks allotted to workshop personnel. Wage structures are based on these work rules and may result in excessive wage costs if flexible dispatching of jobs is to be introduced. Laws and rules of work are designed for the traditional Tayloristic system. Since laws are also designed to be inflexible (which is a sound idea, generally) any adaptation involves a time consuming political process.

5.6 THE SCOPE FOR RESEARCH

Section 5.3 of this chapter introduced a few examples of anthropocentric approaches in manufacturing. However, to assess their impact it is necessary to see them from a holistic point of view, i.e. as a combination of new technologies and new forms of organisation, and with regard to their interaction with the working individual, society as a whole and the environment. This approach calls for interdisciplinary research projects with the intention of formulating an integrated concept of the future factory. The production engineers' task within these interdisciplinary research projects will be to envisage technical implementations. In this context specific research projects will be proposed.

5.6.1 Factory Modelling

Figure 5.9 shows a block diagram of integrated factory modelling and its software functions. It also serves to show possible areas of further development. Present functionality oriented means of description ask for very specific user input. Before a user can build a functional model of a production process he or she must make a comprehensive analysis of the process and boil it down to function primitives. This can be a very demanding task, especially when planning a novel production line. Description means which allow for direct input of data available from previous planning steps, e.g. work plans, geometric models of workpieces and facilities, must be developed.

These data are available from Computer Aided Design (CAD) and Computer Aided Planning (CAP) systems. While standardised protocols for CADCAP (EXAPT Extended Automatic Programming Tools) and CAP-NC programming interfaces (CLDATA - Cutter Location Data, IRDATA - Industrial Robot Data) already exist, there is until now no protocol specification for exchange of geometric and planning data between CADCAP and factory planning. The development of standard protocols for information exchange between the functional modules of a Computer Integrated Manufacturing (CIM) structure is an essential research field. As already seen, information, communication and documentation are instruments for reintegration of activities that used to be performed in partitioned departments, and for delegation of decision making competence to shop floor level. To make free access to and exchange of information possible standardised interfaces must be developed.

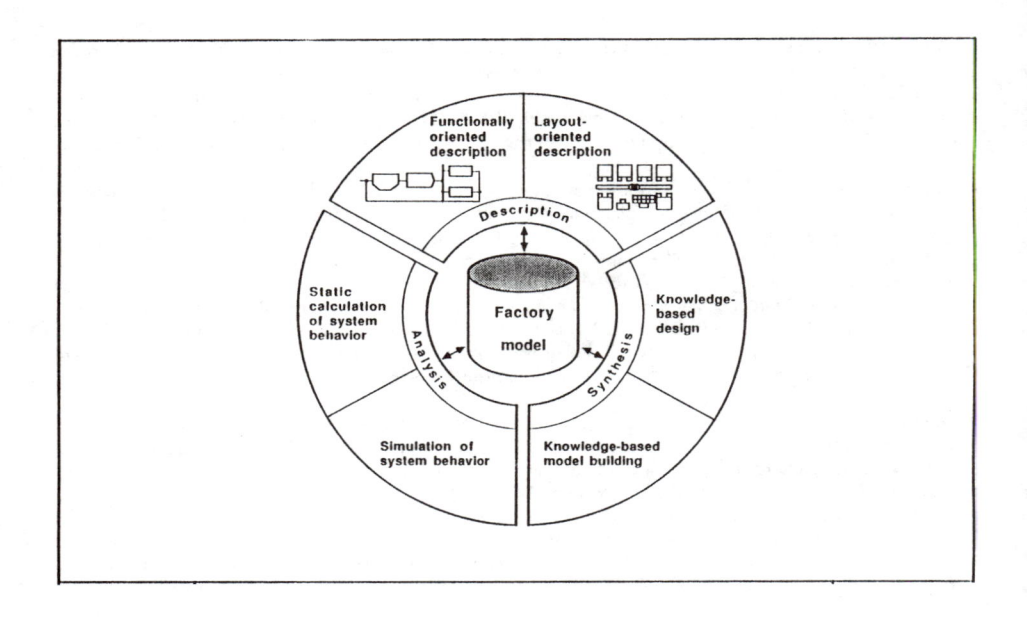

Figure 5.9: Integrated Modelling of a Factory

New knowledge based methods of synthesis must be introduced which will permit generating models of several alternative manufacturing lines from a given functional description. Very comprehensive, though not very detailed knowledge of machining, assembly and other manufacturing tasks as well as facilities which as yet are not available, must be compiled. Novel software will determine suitable combinations of facilities. After the user has made a preliminary selection a knowledge based design module will suggest a layout. Besides, the use of expert knowledge for automated layout design will provide an impetus for the development of CAD.

Improved layout description means will allow for layout models that are 3-dimensional and true to scale. Refined presentation and dialogue functions (man-machine-interfaces) will enable the user to interpret, analyse and manipulate such layout models. Combined with advanced tools for static calculation and dynamic simulation these layout models will give the user a far more clear and realistic picture of an existing or a fictitious manufacturing system than can be achieve today. The planner will have a much greater solution space available, and much clearer criteria as well as far more comprehensive data for evaluating solutions. This will greatly enhance planners' competence and planning quality and thus reduce the risk and cost associated with establishing a new production line. On the other hand the operator will have access to the planning data, insight into the systems design and functionality and means to test the effects of operating decisions beforehand.

5.6.2 Workshop Scheduling

Competence Oriented Workshop Scheduling (COWS) relies heavily on modelling so advances made in the field of factory modelling will be directly beneficial to it. Workshop scheduling must have online connections to machine tools, transport and handling devices and other facilities. On the other hand it needs planning data provided by a Production Planning System (PPS). An integrated production control system combining the functions of PPS, COWS and DNC would meet the objectives of integrating organisational functions, delegating competence to the workshop and reducing the number of management levels.

5.6.3 Knowledge Based Diagnosis

Figure 5.10 shows the architecture of a knowledge based diagnostic system. A future, sophisticated diagnostic expert system will have a knowledge acquisition module with a two tier structure. As much knowledge as possible will be transferred from a comprehensive database that contains general knowledge about products, processes and facilities. The task of selecting valid knowledge from a large database demands a rather powerful expert system in itself. Since this is necessary only once, however, such a configuration module does not have to be part of the diagnostic system itself. The result of this process will be a more or less useful basic system that needs refining for the unique and specific production system it will have to diagnose.

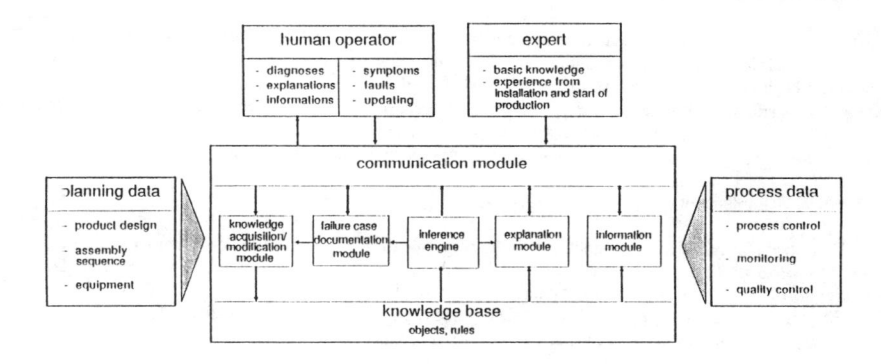

Figure 5.10: Software Structure of a Knowledge Based Diagnostic System

This will be done by analytic methods like Failure Mode and Effects Analysis (FMEA). The knowledge acquisition module will include a software tool supporting this analysis and an editor that permits speedy and efficient input of its results. While FMEA software is available on the market there is no knowledge editor yet. For optimum efficiency this editor will have to be designed with respect to the specific structure of the knowledge base.

In order to make expert systems acceptable to their potential users an explanation module is necessary. Its basic function is to answer the questions 'why' (do you want to know this) and 'how' (did you come to this conclusion). The importance of explanation of the system's functions has been realised early in the development of knowledge based systems, yet there are few practical and no comfortable solutions on the market.

The inference engine is the heart of an expert system. It performs the heuristic search for a solution and infers new hypotheses from established facts by application of procedural knowledge. The design of an inference engine with respect to its tasks and the knowledge it is supposed to operate with is a science in itself and should be left to the information engineers.

An information module will use the knowledge base and additional information on products, processes and facilities to make the function of the manufacturing system transparent to the operator. It will thus enhance both qualification of the user and his decision making competence. A diagnostic system with a powerful information module will be a good addition to factory modelling and workshop scheduling as means of information and communication. If hardware capacity allows it, integration of all three into one computer workstation will result in a very competent information and communication centre on the shop floor.

Modification of the knowledge base will be needed frequently, especially during the start-up phase of a new production line. During this phase the failure rate will be rather high and it is unlikely that all potential faults will have been correctly determined by knowledge acquisition. Adaptation of the production line in the wake of working experience will lead to additional changes to the knowledge base. As far as possible modification should be done by production operators. In order to achieve this a dialogue oriented trace function backed by considerable expert knowledge and sophisticated consistency tests must be introduced.

A communication module will be provided that will support the functions mentioned above by improved input and output functions. The system will have interfaces for access to both planning data and process and machine status data. These will reduce the amount of information the user has to give the system during a failure, i.e. in a situation of great pressure.

5.6.4 Training and Qualification

As stated above the main problem with present training and qualification systems is the clumsy method of user input. Making a computer understand natural speech or hand-sketches may provide for more user-friendly dialogue functions. Both natural speech and geometric modelling have been focal points of research in Artificial Intelligence (AI). Until recently progress has admittedly been slow, mainly owing to the enormous amount of data to be processed. But the exponential increase in computing power we have seen recently, with no end in sight, puts these technologies within the scope of application.

5.6.5 Work Organisation

In order to transfer management functions to the shop floor it is necessary to know what they are in the first place. The tasks allotted to management staff are easily deducted from the organisational structure of a firm. But how do they perform their tasks? What do they actually do? A functional analysis of management jobs similar to that of manufacturing jobs is necessary. After that, a new management structure must be conceived with respect to the potentials of advanced information technology.

5.6.6 Recycling of Materials

The main reasons why so little advance has been made in this field are:

- the great number of different materials in modern consumer goods;

- the difficulty of separating them; and

- the difficulty of identifying them.

Several measures have been suggested to correct this situation. The design of a product must permit easy recycling. This includes a reduction in the number of different materials used, design for ease of maintenance, design for ease of disassembly and efficient use of the material in both product and production process (VDI 1984). New methods for separating materials must be developed and introduced. Experimental disassembly plants have been or will shortly be opened at Leer (Volkswagen AG) and Wackersdorf (BMW AG) for research and development in this field. Chemical marking is being discussed as a means of identifying materials, especially plastics.

5.7 RESEARCH TOPICS WITH ANTHROPOCENTRIC REFERENCES

In the preceding sections a workable definition of the term Anthropocentric Technologies has been found and a few characteristics of their applications have been identified. Now, finally, research topics are formulated within this framework and evaluated in the light of anthropocentric values. The following research projects are proposed:

5.7.1 Factory Modelling

- development of functional description means based on available CADCAP data because this will reduce the amount of routine work and thus enhance creativity of the user;

- development of standard protocols for data exchange between different functional modules within a CIM structure because these will allow for free exchange of data and thus improve perceptibility of production processes;

- compilation of a comprehensive knowledge base for production processes and facilities because this will support decision making competence;

- development of an expert system that generates and evaluates suggestions for facilities and facility combinations from a given functional description because this will permit evaluation of a much larger number of different solutions and thus enhance decision making competence;

- development of a knowledge based automated layout designer because this will free the user from routine work and consequently support his or her creativity;

- development of advanced layout description means that produce true-to-scale 3D-models because this will improve perceptibility of planning data;

- development of advanced presentation and dialogue functions because these will increase the user's freedom of action;

- development of improved tools for static calculation and dynamic simulation because these will improve the data base for planning decisions.

5.7.2 Workshop Scheduling

- development of an integrated production control system because this will enable a reduction in the division of labour.

5.7.3 Knowledge Based Diagnosis

- compilation of a comprehensive knowledge base of fault-symptom relations in products, processes and facilities because this will result in a better understanding of production failures;

- development of a knowledge based configuration module for knowledge based diagnostic systems because this will increase the system operators' competence in fault finding, especially during the start-up phase of a production line;

- development of an efficient expert editor for expert systems because this will reduce the amount of routine work to be done by the expert and enhance his creativity;

- development of an explanation module for expert systems because this will make the working of the expert system understandable to the user;

- development of task-specific information modules for diagnostic systems because these will increase the understanding of the manufacturing system's functions;

- development of a knowledge based, user operated modification module for knowledge based diagnostic systems because this will increase the users freedom of action;

- development of advanced communication functions for knowledge based systems because these will make the user more comfortable with the system.

5.7.4 Training and Qualification

- development of improved input methods using, for instance, natural speech or hand sketches because these will improve user friendliness of the system.

5.7.5 Work Organisation

- functional analysis of management jobs in order to reassess and, consequently, reduce division of labour;
- development of new management structures that utilise information technology to delegate decision making competence to the shop floor and reduce the number of management levels.

5.7.6 Recycling

- study of design features and manufacturing processes that allow for easy disassembly;
- development of consumer goods designed for ease of disassembly in order to reduce waste disposal;
- development of novel methods for separating different materials because this will improve the recycling rate and, thus, utilisation of natural resources;
- development of novel methods for identifying different materials, especially plastics in order to improve the recycling rate.

CHAPTER 6

CONCLUSIONS AND RECOMMENDATIONS

6.1 MAIN CONCLUSIONS

Over the past thirty years some notable changes have occurred in the market place. Price was for many years the most important competitive factor for many manufacturing companies. In this type of economic regime the importance of reducing costs can be understood. In order to remain competitive and profitable, costs must be continually reduced, and the ways in which this objective has been achieved is through mass production (economies of scale), product rationalisation, division of labour, and the use of technology to deskill shop floor employees and to automate production.

During the 1970's the dominance of price competitiveness began to wane, and quality became an equally important competitive factor. However, this did not mean that the need to reduce costs lost any of its force, product price was still important, but the right price alone was not enough because customers were also demanding a high quality product.

During the 1980's a third competitive element started to emerge in manufacturing industry and this was the need to provide customers with greater choice and more customisation. Rapid technological developments also meant that products needed to be continually revised if they were to remain up-to-date. These customer demands, coupled also with the need to reduce costs, have led to a drive to reduce inventory levels. Consequently an extra burden, that of greater flexibility, has now been added to the requirements of reduced costs and improved quality.

World markets are clearly becoming more international, more dynamic and more customer driven, and competition on price alone is no longer a viable business strategy for many manufacturing companies. Other non-price competitive factors have become equally important.

During the 1990's there will be an increasing trend towards tailoring of products to meet customer needs. Although this trend has been described as a move from mass production to one of a kind production, the actual change in market conditions is more complex than this because there will be a whole range of company specific conditions governing strategic choice (Atkinson 1990). Basically the emphasis will be on moving from price competition to quality competition. This can be based on large batches of specialised brand products or on low batches of diversified quality products.

These changes in business strategies do not mean that price competition is dead. In fact there is the opportunity for the most innovative companies to offer a diverse range of low price high quality products.

The important point about these changes in markets is that they have led to a number of trends:

. Reductions in production volumes

. Increased product variety

. Shorter product life cycles (as companies strive to keep their products up to date)

. A reduced number of repeat orders.

These trends are set to continue throughout the 1990's. Opportunities for profit growth will not therefore be derived from economies of scale, but from economies of scope, i.e. competitive advantage will be derived from flexibility rather than from low costs. The key business issues are therefore to reduce manufacturing lead time (including product development time), improve customer service, reduce inventory and increase responsiveness, against a background of highly variable customer demand patterns and changing specifications.

Markets have therefore become more volatile and dynamic, and to remain competitive in these fast changing markets manufacturing companies have to become highly responsive organisations. To survive they will therefore in general, have to achieve, without compromise, three potentially conflicting goals: reduced costs, improved quality and greater flexibility.

The main question that industry and research policy makers will have to address is how will these goals can be achieved and what is an appropriate manufacturing response to these market conditions?

This question is very important. Whilst there is no one single best option that will suit all manufacturing enterprises, it does seem possible to distinguish between two fundamentally different manufacturing responses. One of these is the technological manufacturing response, which is being promoted by the European Commission and many other national research programmes, with the support of industry. The other response is a balanced manufacturing response based on organisation, people and technology, which is being pioneered by a number of far sighted European manufacturing companies (for example the BICC group and Lucas Industries in the UK).

The main conclusion of the report is that the sole pursuit of the technological manufacturing response is wrong, and that a major shift in research policy is required towards supporting the balanced manufacturing response. However, this change of emphasis will have profound implications for engineering design practices.

Many of the established design practices and beliefs used in industry were developed to support a different set of circumstances to those that exist today. In a manufacturing environment that was largely cost driven and based high volume, low variety markets with low levels of competition, it was found that the application of technology to automate production and to deskill the work force produced competitive advantage and made companies more profitable.

The profound changes that have occurred in market circumstances have not however been accompanied by fundamental changes in design practices and beliefs. The design paradigm has remained largely unaltered. This is very characteristic of change situations.

One important conclusion of the report is that the fundamental changes in market conditions discussed in the report not only demand a change in manufacturing response, but also a fundamental shift in design paradigm. Without this shift in paradigm it will not be possible to develop a satisfactory manufacturing response. Paradigm shifts are however difficult to achieve and may be opposed by those who wish to preserve the existing paradigm.

Managers and engineers, like other professional, have a set of core beliefs and assumptions specific and relevant to their profession, which are shared in common with other members of the profession. This is the essence of a paradigm: it is taken for granted and not seen as problematic by those who adhere to it. The paradigm defines how thing are done and what is acceptable.

Paradigms are difficult to change and to challenge because they are more than intellectual they are also political. As a result paradigms tend to slowly evolve as changing circumstances demand, or they or overturned by external agents, e.g. people outside of the paradigm who reject the constructs of the existing paradigm. Alternatively, paradigms can be changed in fundamental ways by internal agents if these people feel confident enough to challenge their own beliefs and to make constructive criticisms of their own past history.

The problems and challenges that are faced by manufacturing today rules out an evolutionary change. However, the revolutionary approach is not appropriate either. Managers and engineers (internal agents), should have the confidence and courage to challenge and to constructively criticise their beliefs and history, and to make some fundamental shifts in their paradigm, calling on external actors for new ideas.

The problem is that many managers and engineers believe that an evolutionary change in design paradigm is needed, and as a consequence they tend to believe that the technological solutions that have worked so well in the past will continue to work. All that is needed is some slight reorientation. This appears to be the basis of the European Commission's response, most notably characterised by the recent interest in human factors and the lack of attention to the way in which manufacturing systems are designed.

It is clear that knowledge of the world is divided into boxes which are man-made and purely arbitrary. There is no natural law which states that the world should be divided into software engineering, industrial psychology, etc. These subjects are of our own making, and the divisions between subjects a matter of convenience. More correctly it should be said that the division of knowledge into these boxes was a matter of convenience. This is no longer the case. In fact it is now a handicap, a barrier to progress.

One of the messages of the report is that engineers should not be using design methods that were developed for market circumstances that no longer exist. It seems that manufacturing design, as with other areas of engineering design, is largely multidisciplinary. Engineers seem to prefer to design technology and then to deal with any problems afterwards, rather than designing technology in a way that avoids any problems. The multidisciplinary method is traditional, but outdated and often ineffective. The way forward lies in interdisciplinary design.

At the moment advanced manufacturing is a very imbalanced activity, because too much attention is paid to technology. It is also largely a multidisciplinary activity. It needs to become an interdisciplinary activity. Technology should be designed to take account of organisation and people considerations.

The big decision for research policy makers is whether they should put all their eggs into one basket. In effect, to gamble the future competitiveness of European manufacturing industry on the belief that there is nothing fundamentally wrong with the traditional technology driven multidisciplinary approach.

The primary focus of the TRN has been upon developing recommendations for future Community funded research in the area of advanced manufacturing based on an interdisciplinary approach to the design of manufacturing systems based on a balance between organisation, people and technology. The emphasis of the recommendations is therefore on organisation and people issues and their impact on technological research. Consideration has been given to recommending changes to existing research programmes such as ESPRIT-CIM and BRITE-EURAM, and identifying topics that would justify establishing new programmes to fill up the gaps.

However, research cannot be considered in isolation from its environment. Community research programmes are normally funded on a shared cost basis with industry. Recommendations for Community actions arising from this Technology Assessment Study must therefore take account of the need to foster greater awareness and to help create an environment that will help the development of research in this area.

As a result it is necessary to provide recommendations for Community actions in:

. Awareness

. Training, and

. Advanced Manufacturing Research.

6.2 AN INTEGRATED APPROACH

Industry is learning that its old approach to manufacturing, which based on separate functional departments, has outgrown its usefulness, and has become a competitive liability. Over the wall manufacturing is slowly being replaced by an integrated approach, the key words being simultaneous activities, coordination, cooperation, sharing, and team working. The European Commission also needs to become more aware that it cannot adequately address the needs of European manufacturing industry without adopting a new organisational approach.

It is evident that manufacturing can no longer be addressed in a simple multidisciplinary way. Many problems in manufacturing need to be resolved in an interdisciplinary manner. It is also evident that existing research programmes do not provide an adequate coverage of manufacturing. Organisation and people issues are under funded and have not had much impact on technological research.

The research issues in advanced manufacturing are much broader and much more interdisciplinary than in the past, and cannot therefore be addressed by any one DG or any one professional group.

The European Commission is therefore strongly recommended to consider developing a European Strategic Research Action in Advanced Manufacturing. It is recommended that this research action build on existing programmes in numerous DG's.

The starting point for research in advanced manufacturing technology should be ESPRIT-CIM and the relevant parts of BRITE-EURAM. Innovation and technology transfer should be addressed by SPRINT. Research in the area of training for advanced manufacturing should be covered by COMETT and DELTA. Any other areas not covered by these five programmes should be addressed by a sixth programme specially created for the purpose. Thus ESPRIT-CIM, the relevant parts of BRITE-EURAM, SPRINT, COMETT and DELTA, and this sixth programme, together should form a European Strategic Research Action in Advanced Manufacturing.

It is important however, that the action be an interdisciplinary one and not multidisciplinary. Thus, for example, questions of user training, technology transfer, motivation etc. must be considered in the development phase and should shape the technology. These issues should be integrated into technological research, and not just left for someone else to deal with after the technology has been developed.

The European Commission will need to consider how this research action should be managed. It is recommended that it be coordinated by a small task force drawn up from Commission staff from the DG's involved in the existing programmes. Care will have to be exercised in the management of the task force, and efforts will have to be expended on creating a team that can overcome loyalties to DG's, divisions and programmes.

It is recommended that the objectives of this new action should be to:

. Assist European manufacturing industry to become more competitive;

. Modernise the technology, organisation, and work practices used by European manufacturing industry;

. Promote European industrial cooperation in precompetitive advanced manufacturing research;

. Develop an interdisciplinary approach to advanced manufacturing.

The research action should address three key themes:

. Advanced manufacturing organisation;

. Advanced manufacturing management and work practices;

. Advanced manufacturing technology.

covering:

. The organisation of the factory;

. Change management techniques;

. Training

. Advanced management and work practices;

. Application of social science;

. Business and manufacturing strategy;

. Interdisciplinary manufacturing systems design;

. Manufacturing accounting techniques;

. IT systems to support people and organisation;

. Technological research.

Some of the existing purely technical research will remain unaffected by the new action. Only those areas which need to be approached in an interdisciplinary way should be changed. There is a need therefore to establish in more detail which areas should be addressed in an interdisciplinary manner.

It is recommended that the workprogrammes of ESPRIT-CIM and BRITE-EURAM should be changed in a way that results in complementary activities within the two programmes. This can be achieved if ESPRIT-CIM focuses on more strategic issues and BRITE-EURAM focuses on more problem and business driven research. Overlap between the two programmes in inevitable, but should be seen as an advantage rather than a source of problems. Overlap ensures a smooth transition from strategic research to applied research and can provide a focus for transferring the results of strategic research into industry.

6.3 AWARENESS

The scope and importance of organisation and people issues in advanced manufacturing are not fully appreciated in industry. There is a tendency to think of human factors, which is perceived to be primarily a quality of working life issue, or is associated with the ergonomics of human-machine interfaces, or training. Moreover, there is an awareness in industry of the need to improve the management of change, but often this tends to be viewed solely as a question of how best to introduce more technology. Also there is a feeling in industry that old demarcations need to be removed and replaced by more flexible work practices. Industry is still largely unaware of the potential improvements in profitability and competitiveness that can be derived from tapping into and mobilising human competence (i.e. skills, judgement, creativity and experience).

There is a need to prepare short and readable awareness material targeted at different groups (e.g. senior managers, engineers, et al.). The aim should be to encourage industry to start to consider for itself the sort of research that should be undertaken. This is something that could be addressed by both FAST and ESPRIT CIM-Europe.

There is a need to alert both European manufacturing and IT industries to the strategic importance and the scope of organisation and people issues, and to help them to identify research themes for the future. This is a task that could be fulfilled by FAST, but not via its usual mechanism of books and reports, which may not be the right vehicle.

Efforts should be made by FAST to reach a wide audience of people involved in developing research policies. There is a need therefore to develop special material suitable for a non-expert audience. It should not be assumed that these non-experts understand the language used by the experts, or that they have the same level of understanding of concepts such as organisation. It is necessary to make some simplifications and to avoid complicating matters with conditional statements, exceptions, etc. The use of intermediary organisations such as trade associations, consultants, professional bodies, etc. should be considered as a means of disseminating information. Special workshops could also be organised in the Member States for the non-expert audience. Such workshops however, should be carefully planned, organised and give the right sort of publicity. There should also be follow up publicity, with workshop reports being circulated to the national press.

ESPRIT CIM-Europe also has a role to play here. It could undertake similar activities. However, since CIM-Europe is better placed to help increase awareness among exiting projects, it recommended that it should concentrate on this area.

There is also a need to transfer to manufacturing industry state-of-the-art know-how on the scope, importance and implications of organisation and people issues so that industry can put the ideas into practice. This is a further task that could be undertaken by CIM-Europe.

The European Commission should also consider increasing the awareness of its technical staff. Technical staff in ESPRIT-CIM and BRITE-EURAM need to be given more time and more opportunities to develop an understanding of organisation and people issues. Training courses should be used, and it suggested that it should be made a condition of employment that technical staff undergo such training.

FAST also needs to reconsider its approach to forecasting and assessment projects. Much useful work has been done by FAST in raising the profile of these issues and identifying the need for more research. FAST now needs to build on this work and move forward. It is therefore recommended that FAST make more use of industrial expertise in the studies that it funds. Industrial input can strengthen the results of projects. FAST should therefore endeavour to expand and to make more use of its network of industrial contacts.

There is also a need for FAST to undertake further forecasting and assessment studies in advanced manufacturing. The economic and financial aspects of advanced manufacturing is one area that needs to be considered. It is evident from the results of the present study that management accounting techniques and financial justification methods are topics that are largely ignored by the technical community. This is without doubt a fruitful area for further investigation.

The education and training of manufacturing systems engineers is also an area that FAST should pay more attention to. There is a need to consider what skills and knowledge engineers should be acquiring from undergraduate courses. At the moment it seems the education of these engineers is firmly rooted in the production engineering culture of the 19th century.

6.4 TRAINING

Training will be a key area for the success of research in the area of organisation and people issues, and the exploitation of research results by industry. There are a number of reasons for this.

First, research is not just a question of addressing organisational and psychological topics in isolation. These also have an impact on technological research, which should now be addressed in an interdisciplinary way. Second, the success of the anthropocentric approach depends to a large extent on the availability of well trained skilled workers.

Manufacturing systems research and design is now an interdisciplinary area. New knowledge and methods of working are needed on the part of engineers. Most engineers do not have the knowledge or skills to work effectively on interdisciplinary research or design projects involving organisation and people issues, but are capable of, and often interested, in acquiring this knowledge.

Demographic changes also imply that greater emphasis needs to be placed on the retraining of older workers. The increasing emphasis that younger people place on quality of working life will also mean that continuing training will have to become the accepted norm if industry is to attract and retain younger workers.

It is recommended that the Commission undertakes within the COMETT and DELTA programmes to assist industry, universities and other colleges to develop appropriate education and training for engineers, managers and craftsmen. Emphasis should be placed on:

. Education and training for a lifetime of learning;

. Developing social skills for group working;

. Learning by doing;

. Increasing links between industry and educational establishments;

. Open learning;

. A psychology of learning driven approach to the development of multi-media learning technologies;

. The training needs of SMEs;

. Broadening of skills and knowledge.

There is a requirement for Interdisciplinary Manufacturing Systems Engineers. The need is to develop training and education material and techniques to broaden the knowledge and experience of engineers at all levels. There is a need to develop design team structures to support interdisciplinary design. What to teach and how to teach is an important question to be resolved. University undergraduate courses need to be revised and training provided for lecturers as well as engineers currently working in industry.

Management competence also needs to be improved. Managers need to be helped to develop a stronger people orientation, and need to become familiar with modern management science theory and practice. Training is also needed to help managers deal with change management and to develop styles of management in keeping with the new emphasis on decentralisation and increased competence on the shop floor.

The training of craftsmen for the computer age also need to be given more serious attention. Flatter hierarchies and decentralisation of decision making towards the shop floor implies increasing competence of shop floor people. Industry does not need machine operators and single skilled craftsmen. The need is for multiskilled computer-aided flexible craftsmen.

The European Commission should work with industry and training organisations to establish what should be taught and how, and then fund the development of the needed material and techniques.

6.5 ADVANCED MANUFACTURING RESEARCH

Attention will be focused in this section on recommending actions that ESPRIT-CIM and BRITE-EURAM can take to build on the proposals for research included in the earlier chapters of this report.

6.5.1 Strategic Issues

Detailed proposals for research are given in Chapters 2, 3, 4 and 5. It is clear from these chapters that there is a consensus on the need for a strategic shift away from automation, especially of decision making, towards using technology to support people. The emphasis of these four chapters in on developing skill supporting rather than skill substituting technologies: technology should be developed which leaves room for the exercise of human skill, judgement and knowledge. Technology should be used to make these distinctive human attributes more productive, and efforts to reproduce these unique characteristics in machines is seen as unproductive, expensive and ultimately futile.

It is also clear that technologists on their own are unlikely to be able to develop skill supporting technologies. The expertise needed lies outside of engineering. Technologists should therefore collaborate with social scientists and address technology as an interdisciplinary subject.

To implement these recommendations a number of strategic changes are needed.

It is recommended that ESPRIT-CIM and BRITE-EURAM adopt the philosophy underlying that of SPRINT action line 'Specific Projects for Intra-Community Innovation Transfers' (Commission of the European Communities 1990) which acknowledges that there is a growing need to adopt a global approach, not a purely technical one. Specific projects are therefore expected to employ an overall systems approach, taking into account all the factors necessary to bring about change. These include technological requirements, management and organisation, training and motivation of staff, etc. Projects should be balanced, addressing elements of organisation, people and technology.

It is important that the ESPRIT-CIM and BRITE-EURAM programmes change their assumptions about organisation and people issues. These are not secondary matters, nor are they issues that should only be dealt with at the implementation stage. They permeate all aspects of manufacturing systems design, including research and development.

It is recommended therefore that it should be assumed that all projects have an organisation and people dimension. It should be left to proposer to demonstrate that this is not the case. It should therefore be made a condition that proposals identify the organisation and people issues and specify how these will be dealt with, or alternatively to demonstrate that organisation and people issues are not relevant. Project evaluation teams should include experts with knowledge and experience of this area. It will be necessary to devise criteria and guidelines to help proposers deal with this aspect of their proposal. It is suggested that these criteria include organisational structure, the role of people, human-computer interaction, ergonomics, motivation, job satisfaction, training, and health and safety. Project evaluators will also need to be given some support with this matter.

It is also important that industrial users give details in the proposal of their organisational structures and practices. The information that they should give needs to be clearly specified. Proposers should be expected to justify their organisational structures and procedures. This should be taken into account during the evaluation.

Once a project is running, project monitoring and formal reviews should pay particular attention to the way that organisation and people issues are being addressed by the consortium.

Another important issue relevant to submission of project proposals is the business and economic justification of projects. It is recommended that industrial users should give an explanation of their business plans and explain what management accounting practices they use. If they are using conventional cost accounting methods, they should explain why they are not using more up-to-date techniques. They should also be asked to give a percentage breakdown of their total manufacturing costs by category (e.g. direct labour, indirect labour, materials, etc.). They should be expected to justify the project with reference to this information. Proposers may need to be given some support with this aspect of the proposal preparation.

Project evaluators should pay particular notice of the financial justification aspects, and should be selected for their knowledge of these issues, not just for their technical expertise. Some support may be necessary to help evaluators with this matter.

The emphasis of ESPRIT-CIM, and to a lesser extent BRITE-EURAM, also needs to shift away from technology-push to market-pull. The emphasis within both programmes should be on the user companies. Vendors should play a secondary role.

6.5.2 Specific Research Recommendations

Research needs to be undertaken on a wide range of topics. Detailed proposals are given in 2,3,4 and 5. It is recommended that ESPRIT-CIM and BRITE-EURAM should give consideration to supporting this research which includes:

- More emphasis on developing IT systems that expand the range of solutions considered by the users of these systems. Single minded emphasis on speed does not make the best use of people or technology.

- Particular emphasis on manufacturing systems design. There is a need for methods and tools to support an interdisciplinary approach, with special emphasis on bottom-up methods, more holistic approaches, appropriate and selective use of technology, increased user involvement, and rapid prototyping.

- The need to address research in manufacturing, not just research into new manufacturing technology. There is a need to develop new management practices, new reward systems, more sophisticated financial justification techniques, new cost accounting methods, etc.

- The development of skill supporting technologies by applying insights form the social sciences. Condition monitoring, free ranging robotic vehicles, database management and networking, applications of genetic algorithms, vision systems, workshop oriented programming of robots and machine tools, decision support systems, computer-aided design, production planning and control systems, etc. are all areas which provide scope for further research with the emphasis on skill supporting technology.

- Research into technologies that will support a shift in market conditions towards one-of-a-kind production (OKP). The success of OKP depends very much on making use of people's intelligence and adaptability and providing the right sort of technology. There is a need therefore to develop technologies that will support this specific approach to manufacturing.

- Technologies to support group working. The increasing emphasis on team or group working demands the development of technologies that will support this way of working. Computer supported cooperative work is therefore an area of research that needs to be considered and addressed.

- Technologies to support the learning company or organisation. This is seen as an important concept for the future. Technologies to support this idea need to be developed.

6.5.3 The Next Steps

Since both ESPRIT-CIM and BRITE-EURAM are industry driven research programmes, industry needs to support the research proposals contained in this report: there is little point in developing workprogrammes that industry will not support. It is recommended therefore that both ESPRIT-CIM and BRITE-EURAM should set up industrial working groups to discuss with industry the contents of this report and the impact that organisation and people issues will have upon these two programmes during the 1990's.

This report should be circulated to members of the ESPRIT Management Committee and the BRITE-EURAM Committee of an Advisory Nature (CAN). Both committees should consider the recommendations of the report and address what action should be taken by the respective programmes.

National Governments should also consider the recommendations of this report because these are also relevant to national research activities. National governments should also seek comments on this report from selected members of their own technical research community and government bodies responsible for funding academic research projects.

It is recommended that any development of new research programmes involving the European Commission, such as the Japanese IMS proposal, should address the issues raised in this report.

It is also recommended that both ESPRIT-CIM and BRITE-EURAM should set up horizontal projects to consider how current research projects can be modified and further developed by addressing organisation and people issues.

In order to achieve a broader understanding and to gain insights in to the way things are developing elsewhere, it is recommended that study tours be organised in the USA to examine how the Americans are addressing organisation and people, and to establish what impact this is having on technological research.

6.5.4 Final Points

Research in the area of manufacturing needs to be addressed in a more interdisciplinary way. Unfortunately, this is not widely appreciated or understood. Research programmes are often structured as if there were no interdisciplinary issues: everything fits into well defined boxes, with no overlap. A general lack of understanding, coupled with a bias towards monodisciplinary research projects, makes it difficult to obtain funding for interdisciplinary projects.

There are therefore barriers, imposed by tradition, that frustrate the attempts of those who want to adopt an interdisciplinary approach. It seems inevitable that research will ultimately become more interdisciplinary. The question is when? The need is already there, but the environment does not foster such approaches.

European researchers were probably the first to realise the importance of interdisciplinary research in manufacturing, and may well have a lead in this area over researchers elsewhere in the world. This lead however can easily be lost if this type of research is not fostered and given adequate funds. The European Commission should avoid a situation arising whereby it lets this valuable research expertise fade away, only to find that it has to start from scratch later on because others have realised its importance.

It is therefore strongly recommended that the European Commission should allocate research funds to foster interdisciplinary research. This type of research should not however be pursued in isolation from established research programmes. The need is to incorporate this approach within ESPRIT-CIM and BRITE-EURAM. It should become an implicit part of projects. However, at the moment this poses difficulties, and there is a need for demonstration projects to pioneer the research methods needed for an interdisciplinary approach. Consequently the question of interdisciplinary design, taking into account issues such as organisation and people should have a high profile.

The European Commission should also note that organisation and people issues in manufacturing will not go away. They will be around for many decades to come, and there are increasing signs that industry is aware of this. However people's enthusiasm has its limits. There are many people who have spent the last ten years trying to get support for their research. On the whole they have failed and they are now starting to feel that they have been wasting their time.

So although the problems may continue to exist for many decades, the same cannot be said for the expertise needed to address these problems. Consequently, if the existing research programmes are not willing to take on board the need to adopt an interdisciplinary approach and to pursue the development of skill supporting technologies, then the European Commission is strongly recommended to establish a new research programme to enable this research to be pursued.

REFERENCES

Ainger, A.W.S., 1990, Aspects of an Experimental Industrial Application of a Human Centred CIM System, Proc. IEE Colloquium on Human Factors in CIM, IEE, London, UK.

Atkinson, J., 1990, Flexibility and Skill in Manufacturing Establishments, IMS Report No 180, Institute of Manpower Studies, Brighton, UK.

Ayres, R.U., 1990, CIM: Hypotheses, Opening Address, IIASA Conference CIM: Revolution in Progress, IIASA, Laxenburg, Austria.

Bainbridge, L., 1983, Ironies of Automation, Automatica, 19, pp 775-779.

Bannon, L.J. and Schmidt, K., 1989, CSCW: Four Characters in Search of a Context, in Proceedings of the 1st European Conference on Computer Supported Cooperative Work, EC-CSCW '89.

Benson, P., Hill, A. and Hoffman, T., 1982, Manufacturing Systems of the Future: a Delphi Study, Production and Inventory Management, 23(3), pp 87-106.

Besant, C.B., Ristic, M., Slatter, R-R., Sahirad, M., Olama, I. and Hatziconstantis, L., 1988 Operation and Management of Flexible Human-centred Turning Cells, Proc. 19th Int. Symposium on Automotive Technology & Automation, Vol. 1, pp 647-678.

Bessant, J. and Haywood, B., 1985, The Introduction of FMS as an Example of CIM, Dept. of Business Management, Brighton Polytechnic, UK.

Blumberg, M. and Gerwin, D., 1984, Coping with Advanced Manufacturing Technology, Journal of Occupational Behaviour, 5, pp 113-130.

Bolk, H., 1989, Management Sciences Contribution to Computer Integrated Manufacturing: Referee, Goal Keeper or First Aid?, In C. Halatsis and J. Torres (Eds.), Computer Integrated Manufacturing, Proc. 5th CIM-Europe Annual Conf., IFS Publications/Springer-Verlag, Kempston, UK.

Bolk, H., 1990, The Benefit or the Doubt: A Strategy for Knowledge Transfer on ESPRIT-CIM Directed at SME's, In L. Faria and W. van Puymbroeck (Eds.), Computer Integrated Manufacturing, Proc. 6th CIM-Europe Annual Conf., Springer-Verlag, London, UK.

Bonsack, R., 1986, Cost Accounting in the Factory of the Future, CIM Review, 2(3), pp 28-32.

Brödner, P., 1984, Group Technology - A Strategy Towards Higher Quality of Working Life. In T. Martin (Ed.), Design of Work in Automated Manufacturing Systems, Pergamon Press, Oxford, UK.

Brödner, P., 1985, Fabrik 2000: Alternative Entwicklungspfade in die Zukunft der Fabrik, Ed. Sigma Bohn, Berlin, Federal Republic Germany.

Brödner, P., 1989, Attempt to Explain the Essence of Anthropocentric Technology", FAST ATA1 Study Discussion Paper, IAT, Gelsenkirchen, Federal Republic Germany.

Browne, J., Harhen, J. and Shivnan, J, 1988, Production Management Systems - A CIM Perspective, Addison Wesley, London, UK.

Bullinger, H.J and Ammer, E.D., 1984, Work Structuring provided the basis for improving the organisation of production systems, Industrial Engineering, 16(10), pp 74-82.

Burbidge, J.J., 1986, Production Planning and Control - A Personal Perspective, IFIP WG 5.7, Munich, Federal Republic Germany.

Burnes, B. and Fitter, M., 1987, Control of Advanced Manufacturing Technology - Supervision without Supervisors? In T.D. Wall, C.W. Clegg, and N.J. Kemp (Eds.), The Human Side of Advanced Manufacturing Technology, John Wiley and Sons, Chichester. UK.

Commission of the European Communities, 1989, Information Package, MONITOR Programme (1989-1992), CEC, Brussels.

Commission of the European Communities, 1990, SPRINT Call for Proposals, Specific Projects for Intra-Community Innovation Transfers, CEC, Brussels.

Chalmet, L.G. 1987 Increasing your Competitive Edge Through CIM. In K. Rathmill and P. MacConaill (Eds.), Computer Integrated Manufacturing, Proc. 3rd CIM-Europe Annual Conf., IFS Publications/Springer-Verlag, Kempston, UK.

Child, J., 1987, Organisation Design for Advanced Manufacturing Technology. In T.D. Wall, C.W. Clegg, and N.J. Kemp (Eds.), The Human Side of Advanced Manufacturing Technology, John Wiley and Sons, Chichester. UK.

Clegg, C., 1988, Appropriate Technology for Manufacturing: Some Management Issues, Applied Ergonomics, 19(1), pp 25-34.

Clegg, C. and Corbett, J.M., 1987, Research and Development into Humanising AMT. In T.D. Wall, C.W. Clegg, and N.J. Kemp (Eds.), The Human Side of Advanced Manufacturing Technology, John Wiley and Sons, Chichester. UK.

Conway, W., Maxwell, W. and Miller, F., 1967, Theory of Scheduling, Addison Wesley, USA.

Corbett, J.M., 1985, Prospective Work Design of a Human-centred CNC Lathe, Behaviour and Information Technology, 4(3), pp 201-214.

Corbett, J.M. 1988, Ergonomics in the Development of Human-centred AMT, Applied Ergonomics, 19(1), pp 35-39.

Cross, K.F., 1984, Production Modules: a flexible approach to high tech manufacturing, Industrial Engineering, 16(10), pp 64-72.

Cummings, T. and Blumberg, M. 1987, Advanced Manufacturing Technology and Work Design. In T.D. Wall, C.W. Clegg, and N.J. Kemp (Eds.), The Human Side of Advanced Manufacturing Technology, John Wiley and Sons, Chichester. UK.

Dempsey, P., 1990, British Industrial Managers' Views on Their Needs in Managing Change Better, Proc. FAMOS Workshop on Human Factors in Assembly, Helsinki, Finland.

Department of Trade and Industry, 1989a, Manufacturing into the Late 1990's, HMSO, London, UK.

Department of Trade and Industry, 1989b, Competitive Manufacturing. A Practical Approach to the Development of a Manufacturing Strategy, IFS Publications, Kempston, UK.

Goldhar, J.D., Wisnosky, D., Hassan, M. and Talaysum, A., 1985, Scale vs. Scope: The Long-Run Economics of the CIM/FMS Factory. In E. Szelke and J. Browne (Eds.), Advances in Production Management Systems '85, North Holland, Amsterdam, The Netherlands.

Grotrian, J. and Seliger, G. 1986, Knowledge and Decision Support for Material Handling Systems. In ESPRIT '86 - Goals and Results. Brussels: Directorate General XIII.

Hamlin, M., 1989a, Human-Centred CIM, Professional Engineer, 2(4), pp 34-36.

Hamlin, M. 1989b, ESPRIT 1199 Deliverable 27, BICC Final Report, BICC Technologies Ltd, Hemel Hempstead, UK.

Hayes, R.H., Wheelwright, S.C. and Clark, K.B., 1988, Dynamic Manufacturing. Creating the Learning Organisation, Free Press, New York.

Hinds, S., 1982, The Spirit of Materials Requirements Planning, Production and Inventory Management, 28(3), pp 35-50.

Holz, B.F., 1984, Economic Evaluation of FMS - a New Approach, Proc. of 3rd Int. Conf. on FMS, IFS (Publications) Ltd, Kempston, UK.

Husband T.M. 1983, Managing Robot Maintenance, 6th BRA Annual Conference, Birmingham, UK.

Jones, B., 1986, Flexible Technologies and Inflexible Jobs - Impossible Dreams and Missed Opportunities, Unpublished Paper, University of Bath, UK.

Jordan, N., 1963, Allocation of Functions Between Man and Machine in Automated Systems, Journal of Applied Psychology, 47(3), pp 161-165.

Kidd, P.T., 1988, The Social Shaping of Technology: The Case of a CNC Lathe, Behaviour and Information Technology, 7, pp 192-204.

Kidd, P.T., 1989, A Note on the Definition of Anthropocentric Systems, Cheshire Henbury Research Report 27, Cheshire Henbury, Macclesfield, UK.

Kidd, P.T., 1990a, Organisation, People and Technology: Towards Continuing Improvement in Manufacturing. In L. Faria and W. van Puymbroeck (Eds.), Computer Integrated Manufacturing, Proc. 6th CIM-Europe Annual Conf., Springer-Verlag, London, UK.

Kidd, P.T., 1990b, Designing CAD Systems: An Open Systems Approach. In W. Karwowski, A.M. Genaidy and S.S. Asfour (Eds.), Computer-Aided Ergonomics, Taylor & Francis, London, UK.

Kidd, P.T., 1990c, An Open Systems Human-Computer Interface for a Workshop Oriented CNC Lathe. In W. Karwowski and M. Rahimi (Eds.), Human Aspects of Hybrid Automated Systems II, Elsevier, Amsterdam, The Netherlands.

Kidd, P.T., 1990d, Information Technology: Design for Human Involvement or Human Intervention? In W. Karwowski and M. Rahimi (Eds.), Human Aspects of Hybrid Automated Systems II, Elsevier, Amsterdam, The Netherlands.

Kidd, P.T., 1990e, Organisation, People and Technology (OPT II): A Method and Toolkit for the Development of a Manufacturing Strategy, Cheshire Henbury Research Report 31, Cheshire Henbury, Macclesfield, UK.

Kidd, P.T., 1990f, Human Factors in CIM: A European Perspective, Proc. IEE Colloquium on Human Factors in CIM, IEE, London, UK.

Kidd, P.T., 1991a, Workshop-Oriented IT Tools for Skill-Based Automated Manufacturing, Proc. Conf. on Information Technology and People, Proceedings of the Open University Conference on Information Technology and People, Open University, Milton Keynes, UK.

Kidd, P.T., 1991b, Interdisciplinary Design of Skill Based Computer Aided Technologies: Interfacing in Depth, International Journal of Human Factors in Manufacturing (to be published).

Kidd, P.T. and Corbett, J.M. 1988, Towards the Joint Social and Technical Design of Advanced Manufacturing Systems, Int. J. of Industrial Ergonomics, 2, pp 305-313.

King, J.R., 1976, The Theory Practice Gap in Job Shop Scheduling, The Production Engineer, March, pp 137-143.

Klingenberg, H. and Kranzle, H., 1987, Humanisation Pays - Practical Models, Volume 2 Production and Production Control, RKW, Eschborn, Federal Republic Germany.

Latham, D., 1981, Are you among MRP's walking wounded?, Production and Inventory Management, 22(3), pp 33-41.

Lawrence, A., 1986, Are CAPM systems just too complex?, Industrial Computing, September, p 5.

Leonard, R., 1988, Elements of Cost-effective CIM, Int. J. Computer Integrated Manufacturing, 1(1), pp 13-20.

Marsden, A.W., 1986, The Management of Change to Advanced Technology - Considering the Human Factors, Proc. of 3rd Int. Conf. on Human Factors in Manufacturing. IFS (Publications) Ltd., Kempston, UK.

Meredith, J.R., 1987, Automating the Factory: Theory Versus Practice, Int. J. Prod. Res., 25(10), pp 1493-1510.

Metalworking Production, 1988, The Sixth Survey of Machine Tools and Production Equipment in Britain, Morgan Grampian, London, UK.

Nadler, G. and Robinson, G. 1987 Planning, Designing and Implementing AMT. In T.D. Wall, C.W. Clegg, and N.J. Kemp (Eds.), The Human Side of Advanced Manufacturing Technology, John Wiley and Sons, Chichester. UK.

Nanda, R., 1986, Redesigning Work Systems a new role for the IE (industrial engineer), Proceedings of the 1986 Fall Industrial Engineering conference, AIIE, pp 222-229.

Northcott, J., Brown, C., Christie, I., Sweeney, M. and Wallington, A., 1986, Robots in British Industry, Policy Studies Institute, London, UK.

Paterson, T.T. 1977, Job Evaluation, Business Books.

Peters, T.J. and Waterman, R.H., 1982, In Search of Excellence. Lessons form America's Best-Run Companies, Harper and Row, New York.

Rosenbrock, H.H., 1984, Designing Automated Systems: Need Skill be Lost?. In P. Marstrand (Ed.), New Technology and the Future of Work and Skills, Frances Pinter, London, UK.

Rosenbrock, H.H. (ed.), 1989, Designing Human-Centred Technology. A Cross-Disciplinary Project in Computer-Aided Manufacturing, Springer-Verlag, London.

Safizadeth, M. and Raffat, F., 1986, Formal/informal Systems and MRP Implementation, Production and Inventory Management, 27(1).

Schneiderman, A.M., 1986, Optimum Quality Costs and Zero Defects: are they contradictory concepts, Quality Progress, November, pp 28-31.

Seliger, G., Baur, P., Bollmann, O. and Kaase, W., 1989, Wissensbasierte Diagnose in der Montage, Montage, 1(3).

Shingo, S., 1981, Study of the Toyota Production System from an Industrial Engineering Viewpoint, Japanese Management Association.

Sorg, A., Hartman, G., Warner, M. and Nicholas, I., 1983, Microelectronics and Manpower in Manufacturing, Gower, Aldershot, UK.

Spur, G., Seliger, G. and Eggers, A., 1982, Dialogue Oriented Workshop Order Scheduling in Flexible Automated Manufacturing. Proceedings of the 23rd International Machine Tool Design and Research Conference, Manchester, UK.

Stark, J., 1988, Organisation, People and Technology - Complementary Components for Successful use of CADCAM, Int J. of AMT, 3(1), pp 3-13.

Taylor, F.W., 1902, Shop Management, Transactions American Society of Mechanical Engineers, 24, pp 1337-1480.

Taylor, F.W., 1907, On the Art of Cutting Metals, Transactions American Society of Mechanical Engineers, 28, pp 31-350.

VDI (1984), VDI 2243 Recyclingorientierte Gestaltung Technischer Produkte, VDI-Verlag, Düsseldorf, Federal Republic Germany.

VDI (1989), VDI 3780 Empfehlungen zur Technikbewertung (Entwurf), VDI-Verlag, Düsseldorf, Federal Republic Germany.

Voss, C.A., 1988, Success and Failure in Advanced Manufacturing Technology, International Journal of Technology Management, 3(3), pp 285-297.

Warnecke, H.-J., 1988, Computer Integrated Manufacture, Computer Integrated Manufacturing Systems, 1(1), pp 6-12.

Wieneke-Toutaoui, B., 1987, Rechnerunterstütztes Planungssystem fur Auslegung von Fertigungsanlagen. Wien: Carl Hanser Verlag, München, Federal Republic Germany.

Williamson, I.P., 1989, Integrated Manufacturing: Developing your Strategy. In C. Halatsis and J. Torres (Eds.), Computer Integrated Manufacturing, Proc. 5th CIM-Europe Annual Conf., IFS Publications/Springer-Verlag, Kempston, UK.

APS RESEARCH PAPER SERIES

APS Series, General Editors: Tony Charles and Werner Wobbe, FAST - Brussels.

Editors (from the main contractors): Stefan Van Bandemer and Josef Hilbert, Institut Arbeit und Technik, Wissenschaft Centrum NordRhein Westfallen, Gelsenkirchen, Germany.

GENERAL ISSUES

1. W. Wobbe: "What are Anthropocentric Production Systems and why is this an issue for Europe?"

2. D. Brandt: "Advanced Experiences with APS".

3. P. Kidd: "Organisation, People and Technology in Europe Manufacturing".

4. F. Lehner: APS: The European Response to Advanced Manufacturing and Globalisation. Synthesis Report.

5. F. Rauner: "Industrial Cultures in the US, Japan, Germany, France and Relation to APS (Synthesis Report from the CAPIRN Network).

6. S'O Siochru: "Prospects for APS in Less Industrialised Member States"

REPORTS ON THE SOCIO-ECONOMIC ASSESSMENT FOR APS IN THE EUROPEAN COMMUNITY FROM THE IAT NETWORK:

Prospects for Anthropocentric Production Systems in:

7. GERMANY: S. V Bandemer, J. Hennig, J. Hilbert, IAT

8. UNITED KINGDOM: T. Charles, R. Charles, A. Roulstone, Staffordshire Polytechnic.

9. FRANCE: D. Linhart, CNRS-GIP, "Mutations Industrielles".

10. ITALY: O. Marschisio, Studio Giano.

11.	DENMARK:	L. B Rasmussen, Technical University of Denmark, B. Clematide, P. Banke, Danish Technological Institute.
12.	NETHERLANDS:	B. Dankbaar, MERIT.
13.	BELGIUM:	a. General Report P. Berckmans, E. Eysackers, STV b. Textiles and Clothing Industry E. Eysackers, STV
14.	IRELAND:	S. O'Siochru, B. Dillon, NEXUS
15.	SPAIN:	O. Homs, CIREM, F. Mana, ICT
16.	PORTUGAL:	I. Kovacs, A. Brandao Moniz, A Mateus, CESO
17.	GREECE:	Z. Papadimitriou, University of Thessaloniki
18.	UNITED STATES:	R. Gordon, J. Krieger
19.	JAPAN:	Y. Masuda
20.	GERMANY:	F. Rauner, K. Ruth
21.	FRANCE:	M. Liu, H. Viala, Paris.
22.	AUSTRALIA	R. Badham

DESIGN AND TECHNOLOGY RELATED CONTRIBUTIONS TO APS

23.	F. den Hertog:	"Anthropocentric Technology Design, Development and Diffusion".
24.	O. Danielsen:	"Human Centredness and Expert Systems".
25.	H. Hirsch-Kreinsen, C. Köhler, M. Moldaschl, R. Schultz-Wild (ISF):	"Technological Preconditions for Skilled Production Work in Computer Integrated Manufacturing".
26.	V. Eichner:	"Organisational Concepts in German Industry".
27.	H. Gottschalch:	"Methods and Processes of Work-orientated Design in CIM Structures".

For up-to-date information on European Community research

consult

CORDIS
The Community Research and Development Information Service

CORDIS is an on-line service set up under the VALUE programme to give quick and easy access to information on European Community research programmes.

The CORDIS service is at present offered free-of-charge by the European Commission Host Organisation (ECHO). A menu-based interface makes CORDIS simple to use even if you are not familiar with on-line information services. For experienced users, the standard Common Command Language (CCL) method of extracting data is also available.

CORDIS comprises eight databases:

- RTD-News: short announcements of Calls for Proposals, publications and events in the R&D field
- RTD-Programmes: details of all EC programmes in R&D and related areas
- RTD-Projects: containing 14,000 entries on individual activities within the programmes
- RTD-Publications: bibliographic details and summaries of more than 50,000 scientific and technical publications arising from EC activities
- RTD-Results: provides valuable leads and hot tips on prototypes ready for industrial exploitation and areas of research ripe for collaboration
- RTD-Comdocuments: details of Commission communications to the Council of Ministers and the European Parliament on research topics
- RTD-Acronyms: explains the thousands of acronyms and abbreviations current in the Community research area
- RTD-Partners: helps bring organisations and research centres together for collaboration on project proposals, exploitation of results, or marketing agreements.

> For more information and CORDIS registration forms, contact
> ECHO Customer Service
> CORDIS Operations
> BP 2373
> L-1023 Luxembourg
> Tel.: (+352) 34 98 11   Fax: (+352) 34 98 12 34

If you are already an ECHO user, please indicate your customer number.

European Communities – Commission

EUR 13967 — Organization, people and technology in European manufacturing

P. Kidd

Luxembourg: Office for Official Publications of the European Communities

1992 — XV, 103 pp., num. tab., fig. — 14.8 x 21.0 cm

Science and technology policy series

ISBN 92-826-3819-7

Price (excluding VAT) in Luxembourg: ECU 12

This report contains the results of a study aimed at identifying proposals for future research funded by the European Commission addressing the issues of organization, people and technology in the area of advanced manufacturing. The primary objective of the study was to develop recommendations for research, with emphasis on the issues of organization and people and their impact on technological research.